# The
# ARKANSAS
# LAWYER

# The
# ARKANSAS
# LAWYER

TERRY DRUYVESTEIN

**ARPress**
ILLUMINATING IDEAS
EMPOWERING VOICES

**ARPress**
45 Dan Road Suite 5
Canton, MA 02021

Hotline:1(888) 821-0229
Fax:      1(508) 545-7580

Ordering Information:
Quantity sales. Special discounts are available on quantity purchases by corporations,associations, and others. For details, contact the publisher at the address above.

Printed in the United States of America.

| ISBN-13: | Softcover | 979-8-89356-737-3 |
|----------|-----------|-------------------|
|          | eBook     | 979-8-89356-738-0 |

Library of Congress Control Number: 2024908966

# TABLE OF CONTENTS

# ACKNOWLEDGEMENTS

I wish to thank my wife, Loretta for having had the patience to see me through the process of putting my thoughts into words for the Arkansas Lawyer. I wish to thank my siblings; Karen Spring, Donna Palmer, Mike Druyvestein of Custer, South Dakota and Virginia Steenson of Stanford, Nebraska who reviewed my initial writings and encouraged me to continue on. I give a special thanks to my life-long friends who graciously read my draft and also encouraged me to finalize the Arkansas Lawyer: Ken and Barb Hoff of Forest Lake, Minnesota who were close college friends and room mates many years ago but who still keep in touch. Also Herb and Jean Hannich of Missoula, Montana, with whom we have experienced many adventures.

I especially thank the attorneys, Jaclyn and Justin Daake of Alma, Nebraska who graciously read my drafts and made very constructive comments on how to improve the Arkansas Lawyer from both a legal and readability standpoint.

# PROLOGUE

Some 2000 years ago a judge, a Roman governor by the name of Pilate, asked his accused, named Jesus of Nazareth, "Are you a king?" Jesus answered, "For this I was born, I have come into the world to bear witness to the truth, everyone who is of the truth listens to my voice." Pilate responds, "What is truth?" To a Christian, Jesus tells the truth. To the Jewish leaders of that day, it is not the truth.

Truth has to be absolute, known fully, if only perhaps by a deity. Jesus said that He came into the world to bear witness to the truth. It is important for us then, as human beings, to know that someone knows the "truth." Someone has to have a complete understanding of what the truth is. It is important for a human being, who has been falsely accused and put in prison, to eventually be set free by the truth. I don't mean only set free from the bars of prison, but also set free from the crime one has falsely been convicted of. That person has a need to know that the truth is not lost, that the truth will eventually come out, that someone or some deity knows the truth and the truth will set him free.

Honesty is often closely associated with truth. An honest person is often defined as one "who tells the truth." But, honesty is sometimes true and it sometimes is not. An eye witness, as an example, may tell the truth as he/she sees it, but eyewitnesses are notoriously mistaken. Honesty has more to do with our human trait as to how "we" honestly see the truth rather than what the truth actually is. Absolute truth then— that known only to God – is often not known to man, but we still havethis inner desire and strive to find it.

So why is truth of such importance? What is it important for? Is truth important to a judge or a jury so that justice may be served? Justice, at least real justice, can only be served if one has the "true" facts and the adjudicator listens to these "true" facts. This is why witnesses swear, often with their hand on the Bible, that they will "tell the truth, the whole truth, and nothing but the truth, so help me God." So why swear "so help me God"? It is because we acknowledge that only God knows real truth and we implore Him to help us tell that truth to the best of our ability. Truth then is the cornerstone of our justice system. Without finding the truth, a judge cannot deliver justice.

We often hear that a person commits some damaging act "because it is legal to do so." We now live in a society where the measure for doing almost anything is whether it is "legal to do so." That is not good enough. There never can be enough laws written to regulate all actions in a society. When I was a young man I watched my father complete many construction projects mostly for farmers in South Dakota, by simply shaking their hands and saying, "OK we have an agreement." Honesty and being truthful were "badges of honor" and if a business person especially were not truthful, he would soon be found lacking in moral character and would not be able to stay in business. This was a great system, at least for small contracts, and it still serves many people in many ways. Now many things are more complex and as a result we work under a "legal system" where everyone has their own attorney who draws up a legal contract, often with lots of fine print, and the standard of measure is "if something is legal" and not "if something is fair." For the old system to work, both parties had to be fair and truthful with each other and remain so. Yes, there were then, as there are now, crooks – business crooks and also consumer crooks, but I often wonder if we would not be better off without all the disclaimers, legal language, and weasel wording now used in almost every agreement. Because of our perception that "if it is legal, it has to be OK" we are trapped into a situation that we hide behind what is legal to guard against what is true. Yes, our legal profession often uses the legality of the law to prevent the truth from prevailing rather than to aid in finding the truth. You will find in this book people doing exactly that.

I would like to examine our justice system. In the U. S. we often say that "our system of justice may not be perfect, but it is the best there is." I have to say that attitude sets the bar too low. Our legal system is not so perfect that we should not always be striving to improve it. I see many things which are legal only because there is a law on the books that makes it so for a special interest. Sometimes these laws need to be brought into question. Sometimes these laws, seemingly good at first, end up being badly abused. The bottom line is that we, as a society, need to be vigilant in keeping our laws fair and equitable, especially in these times of the electronic or computer age. How we do things is changing day by day. We have records of things that we never could have dreamed of before: GPS records of one's location, telephone records, banking records at a fingertip – all this information which can be used to find the truth or to hide the truth. This is a moving target which always needs to be scrutinized. In this book you will find outdated laws which were a hindrance rather than a friend of justice.

We, as humans, need to have an avenue for getting justice. As I alluded to previously, I would say that this is a special human trait. Well, it is specifically in our human DNA and it is not found in other creatures. A sense of justice is reserved for the human race. They say that a dog "is man's best friend". A dog does not need justice to serve mankind. If you don't agree, just take your dog and your wife or other close friend, and lock them in the trunk of your car and drive around for a couple of hours. Then open the trunk and see which one wags its tail and is glad to see you. The dog just wants to be your friend, no matter how you treat it. Your spouse on the other hand, will seek justice and you will learn an expensive lesson. This is an example only; don't ever lock your spouse in the trunk. If you do not recognize this, it is a legal disclaimer.

Webster defines justice as the administration of what is "just" by assigning merited rewards or punishments. Also the administration of the law. Fairness and righteousness. So, in a just society, we look to our laws for fairness and truthfulness. Our laws must be fair and equitable to all. We depend on witnesses to tell the "truth." This is why we are sworn in to "tell the truth, the whole truth, and nothing but the truth, so help me God." For our system of justice to work, we must tell the truth. I need to introduce myself. My name is Terry; I was born in 1941 when our country was entering WWII. I am now 79 years old, but this story is not about my life. It is a story however, that spans all of my life, from some of my first memories as a child up until now as I write this account. It is a story about my father and the relationship he and our family had with his brother. It is about wishes and requests they each made of me at the end of their lives and how those wishes played out. It is a story about how "what is legal" can run contrary to finding justice. It is about people tied together by family bonds who cannot find justice because of the elusiveness of a little thing called "truth." It's also about the justice system and how truth or the lack thereof, can prevent justice from being served. It is about how our justice system often favors the legality of matters and as a result falls woefully short in finding the truth.

This is a true story. As it is often said, "There are just some things you can not make up." You may wonder how things could, by chance or even design, happen as they did. But I assure you that the facts are true and you often will have to draw your own conclusions, reading between the lines, to determine if things happened by chance or if someone was behind the scene, influencing the outcome. First, I will have to give you some background on the people and their wishes. Secondly, throughout the entire story, I will give you my layman's opinion on how the "law" is not synonymous with "justice" and how in actual practice we must have truth to get justice. I will attempt not to bore you with technicalities of the law as I am not a lawyer and do not have their same understanding of what constitutes justice. The legal profession looks at getting justice, under the law. I look at justice as what is received when the truth is known. I believe I am a person of good common sense and I know right from wrong, just as I believe most people in our country know this but unfortunately do not always practice it. I will invite you to think about what the "truth" is and what justice should be if greed and envy did not derail the system.

I said I am an honest person. Perhaps I equate honesty with fairness. Do you consider yourself an honest person? A fair person? I think most of us do. Would you go back into the store where you just finished shopping to return a dollar to the clerk who gave you too much change back? Is it important to you? It should be important to us all because that is the bedrock of fairness. It is not the dollar after all, rather it is the principal of the thing. A clerk gave you too much change back and it is not rightfully yours. Obviously it is not worth your time to interrupt your schedule for a measly dollar, but it is the right thing to do and I wish more people would just do it because "it is the right thing to do." I once got $100 in extra bills when getting some cash at the bank. Now this was serious money when it happened. Did I bring it back? Well yes, I just whipped back through the drive thru lane and told the clerk, "You did not give me the correct change for my check." At first she was a little bit miffed for being accused of making a mistake. When I told her that "No, you gave me a $100 extra," she was more congenial. She thanked me very much as she said it would have come out of her salary when she totaled up at the end of the day. You will see when reading this book that I do not particularly like bankers. But I do like people, principled people mainly, and I think we need to treat each other fairly and respectfully even when we do not agree with each other.

Did I tell you that I am an engineer? No, I'm not talking about one that drives a train. I'm a civil engineer, or at least that was my profession for about 50 years. I still work a little, operating a drinking water and sewage treatment plant for the subdivision I live in. Well, I have a little story about a "mechanical engineer", but it makes my point as to how we perceive different professions.

There was this mechanical engineer who died, I suppose of old age, and rises up to where he sees St. Peter at the Pearly Gates. Well, seems that St. Peter looks and looks through the records and can not find his name. The engineer, now becoming quite nervous, asks, "What does this mean, you not finding my name in the records?" St. Peter says, "Well this means that you must go down there, you know, where Satan and hell are." So that is what happens. Well, things become unusually quiet in hell and when hell gets quiet, St. Peter gets nervous about it so he calls down to talk with Satan. He says, "Things are quiet down there Satan, not as much crying and gnashing of teeth as usual." Satan says, "Well we got this new guy down here, a mechanical engineer, and he has made us a water cooler which has provided us with water to quench our thirst and cool our tongues and now he is working on a series of air conditioners to cool things down a little more. Yes, things are looking better." Well, St. Peter says, "That must have been a mistake! The engineer should never have been sent down there, send him back up here." Satan says, "No, you sent him here and we are keeping him." St. Peter says, "Well, it had to be a mistake in the records, send him back up here or I'll sue!" "Yeah," Satan says, "and where are you going to get a lawyer?"

If you are a lawyer you may say, "That is a horrible joke," but also you have probably heard it before. Why is that? It is because attorneys have gained a bad reputation for honesty and telling the truth, and unfortunately, it is at least in part deserved. It is deserved because there are too many in the legal profession who stifle the truth by "hiding behind the law." It should be the other way around; we should be using the law to find the truth. It has not always been this way. Lawyers and judges in particular were highly respected professions when our country was founded. While still respected by many, there is a continuing erosion of confidence in our legal system and those who run it.

To be honest, or at least fair, the lawyers are only part of the problem. Society demands the services of lawyers far too much and we are far too litigious. It seems that we should be much quicker to settle our affairs without a legal battle in a court of law. Most of the time, neither party wins. Both lose in terms of money, sleepless nights and unforgiving attitudes.

x

If everyone told the truth, the job of dealing out "justice" would be quite easy, don't you agree? Well, at least it would be a lot easier than it is. Why is that? Witnesses swear to tell the truth, but on the other hand, they may even be coaxed by others who look at their job as one of winning and not as one of finding the truth. Witnesses are told, or at least we hear that they are told, not to lie. To lie, under oath, would be perjury. But on the other hand, it may be acceptable to put a little "spin" on what they say. Our politicians are masters at this. Often times there is so much "spin" one can not possibly distinguish truth from an outright lie. This is a pathetic political climate we are living in. If a judge or juror can no longer expect that a witness is telling the truth, how can justice be served? I say "no longer" as if I am implying that people are not as truthful today as they used to be. I am more referring to our country's leaders who are definitely not as honest as they once were. There used to be "statesmen", people of high moral character, and we looked to them with respect, not only for their "personal example" they set for us, but also out of respect for the position they held. I can hardly think of a single politician I could now call a statesman. These are our leaders, examples to our justice system, and most are lawyers. How can we succeed as a just nation when we have such poor examples to follow?

The politicians who dominated the news this past year were the ones conducting the impeachment hearings in preparation for the trial of President Donald Trump. The politicians were in their glory, both sides of the aisle, but mainly in the House where Jerry Nadler was chairman of one of the house committees. I noticed that during this hearing, Representative Nadler was questioned as to why the witnesses were not being sworn in on the Bible and asked to repeat the oath to tell the truth, the whole truth, "so help them God." I don't remember who challenged the chairman but Representative Nadler's retort will stick with me for a long time. He said that he was no longer asking people to swear on the Bible because it was not necessary and that it made some people uncomfortable to do so. Well, why would it be uncomfortable to do so? I guess that by taking an oath and asking our Creator to help one remember and truthfully answer questions is insulting to some! The drafters of the Declaration of Independence and the U. S. Constitution were mostly people who believed in a God. Thus it starts out, "We hold these truths to be self-evident, that all Men are created equal, that they are endowed by their Creator with certain unalienable Rights, that among these are Life, Liberty, and the Pursuit of Happiness." I think to honor the statesmen who put their life on the line to form our Constitution and to recognize in our founding documents the existence of our Creator is ample enough reason to carry on our tradition of saying an oath to God before giving testimony. Truth is important, "so help me God."

# CHAPTER ONE

## The Family

It was a hot and clear spring day in Ft. Smith, Arkansas when my wife Loretta and I got off the plane and walked across the tarmac to be greeted by my uncle Humpy. As we shared a big hug, Humpy said, "I am so sorry I did not loan you the money when you needed it." I immediately knew what he was referring to and answered, "That's OK Humpy, we got by and things turned out OK." What he was referring to had happened 25 years before and we had not seen each other in person in all those years. We had kept in touch over the years with sporadic phone calls and of course Christmas cards, but we never discussed the request I had made of him after my father, his brother Tom, had passed away two and a half decades BEFORE. For him to start our long overdue face to face reunion with those words was, to put it mildly, a very serious utterance, something which must have troubled him deeply.

Herman John was always called "Humpy" by our family and his close friends in Arkansas. He was H. J. Druyvesteyn to his business associates in the construction industry. Humpy and my dad Tom were always close brothers. Tom was born in 1918 and Humpy in 1921 and both worked in the heavy construction industry throughout their lives. They worked together for Western Contracting out of Sioux City, Iowa in the years leading into World War II. Both grew up near Rock Valley, Iowa and Tom was the first to land a job with Western. Tom was well thought of and was able to help his brother get on the crew as an equipment operator. Tom was married to Ione, and they had started a family while Humpy was single when they went to Ft. Smith to work on Camp Chaffee. The government was in dire need to build military training camps and contractors were in high demand who could get the job done in quick order. Long hours with little housing available is what the men faced when working on these camps. Tom bought a 16-foot travel trailer and that is where he housed his family, consisting of his wife Ione and two children, Yvonne and Donald, ages one and three. In 1940 they completed site grading and infrastructure work on Camp Chaffee and moved on to the construction of Ft. Leonard Wood in Missouri. It was there in 1941 where I was born.

After Ft. Leonard Wood, both Humpy and Tom joined the army to help fight for their country. Humpy went in first and fought in the European theater. With three children, Tom went in later and fought in the Pacific and found action in the liberation of the Philippines, Luzon and the Pyukyus. Tom was discharged in 1946 after attaining the rank of Master Sergeant.

After the war, Humpy returned to Arkansas where he went back to construction work. Tom returned to South Dakota where his family was spending the war years near his wife's parents, John and Nellie Buckles in Corsica, South Dakota. The earliest memory of my life was when my father came home from the war in 1946. I would have not quite been five years old but I distinctly remember this man with a uniform coming to our home and causing a tremendous upset in our way of life. Tears of happiness perhaps, but more anxiety than I could take without it impacting my memory. The other thing that I remember – and it happened close to the same time – were memorial services at the Corsica cemetery where my mother and my grandparents were crying and very upset. This was because my mother had lost a brother and my grandparents their oldest son. Alan Buckles was killed in action in the Pacific. He had been wounded and sent back to a hospital for recovery. He had not wanted to leave his unit but had sent word that he was OK and looked forward to returning home. My grandparents had joyfully received this word and were then stunned to learn shortly afterward that the Japanese had bombed the hospital and Alan had been killed.

Following the war, the brothers followed their separate lives. Having returned to Arkansas, Humpy married a Southern girl named Virginia Helms and started his own construction business working mostly with earth moving equipment. Tom settled into mechanic and blacksmithing work in his wife's home town of Corsica, South Dakota. He now had four children as Karen was born to the family in 1944. In 1947, because of his exceptional skills and training with mechanics and welding, Tom was contacted by Western Contracting, who he had worked for prior to the war. He was to work as a mechanic for a contract they held to complete the earthwork on Ft. Randall Dam constructed on the Missouri River. The location of the dam was not too far west of Corsica so he accepted. This would be the second dam on the Missouri River and it still backs up the 11th largest reservoir in the United States. Ft. Randall was to be an earth fill dam and the work fit well with Western Contracting and Tom's experience with earth working equipment. Tom would eventually become their head equipment superintendent, in charge of maintaining all equipment including draglines, shovels, Euclid trucks, scrapers, crushers and river dredges. The project was a key initial player in a series of dams to be constructed under the Pick-Sloan Plan for the Missouri River. It was authorized by The Flood Control Act and would take several decades to fully complete.

There would now be six children in our family, adding Donna in 1947 and Mike in 1951. The seventh and last, Virginia would be born in 1955. In 1952, our family moved to a home in southeast South Dakota, located on the shores of a waterfowl refuge which was called Lake Andes. We now would be only three miles from the town of Lake Andes, and my father would be 24 miles closer to his work on Ft. Randall Dam. The family went to school in the small town of Ravinia where some of the dam's workers could find housing. I remember a student one year ahead of me by the name of Tom Brokaw. He went on to make a name for himself as a National TV news person. If you are old enough you will recognize who this is. His father was also working on the dam.

It was in Corsica and Lake Andes that I especially remember the close relationship of my dad and his brother Humpy. Humpy would come and visit every year during the South Dakota pheasant hunting season. The brothers loved to hunt and fish. It was a good common interest which held many families together. South Dakota pheasant populations were high and the hunting was good. There were several relatives near Corsica who had farms and abundant pheasants which they would share. The men joked and ribbed each other when one would miss a shot. They would impress a small youth who wanted to hunt but was at first too young to do so. But, I often went along to learn from them and to learn how to eat noon lunch in the field with bratwurst and mustard sandwiches, and Vienna sausages, sardines, cheese and salami, also pickled pig's feet and all kinds of things my mother would never feed me. I can still smell the smoke from the shotgun discharges and especially the dogs, the fields and the birds. Life was good and the brothers were as close as they could be in times when working was everything and recreation was secondary.

We were a big family with seven kids. We were a poor family by most standards but most of the families in our area were not by any means rich either. The kids either didn't care or more likely, no one really noticed that much about your "poor" appearance – when you rarely showed up with a "new piece" of clothing to wear. We loved to see Humpy and his first wife Virginia come – I am not certain it was because we liked them so much, as Humpy was a fun guy and loved to tease us kids – but perhaps also that they would always bring us kids some presents. Humpy and Virginia did not have children and could not have any – so they treated us kids and we loved it. My sisters remember Humpy talking to my dad once as he said – "Tom, you may not be rich in dollars, but you sure are rich with family." That was a good compliment by any standard, and when I now look back I can certainly see how it was true.

When the earth work on Ft. Randall was completed in late 1953, my dad started his own excavation business. It was a tough business and hard to make a good living. We also had a bait business at the lake and a carpenter friend built some wood boats for us to rent. It was a great place to grow up among grass roots people and great fishing and bird hunting. But Tom wanted the best for his family and when Humpy asked him to come to Arkansas to work with him, he consented. Humpy said he had lots of work and that Tom should be able to make a go of it in Ft. Smith, Arkansas. So in September of 1955 our family packed all of our belongings, closed the doors on the house at Lake Andes, and moved to Ft. Smith.

My family had a hard time adjusting to the "Big City" life in Ft. Smith. Don, the oldest son went to work driving a truck for Humpy. Yvonne was a Junior in the high school. I was a 9th grader in Ramsey Junior High. Karen and Donna were in the elementary school. We did not adjust too well into our new environment. I can only speak for myself when I say that I had a hard time adjusting to a school with over 2,000 students. Coming from Ravinia where my class had about 20 students, I was overwhelmed. Ramsey was a "segregated school," a condition which I had no prior knowledge of. The first day I went to class, my cousins Jimmy and Jerry Helms showed me around. They showed me where I could go and where I should not. There were gangs and there was an authority order within the gangs, and the non gang kids such as myself needed to stay out of the way. You stayed away from trouble by staying clear and I had to be careful not to insult anyone. We had our own "cool guy" to pattern after. His name was Donald Bolton. He rode a Harley and wore a white tee shirt and a leather jacket. He had the easy "swagger" which set him apart from all us "dorks" so we idolized him and in many ways tried to no avail to imitate some of his mannerisms, – like rolling up your cigarette package in your tee shirt sleeve.

I survived my first year of school but was happy to be free for the summer. I had experienced segregation but had not learned the lesson. We were living on the outskirts of Ft. Smith near Barling and the area was rural at that time. There was a local gas station where kids would gather to play the pin ball machine. It was the Highway 22 Store. In the store there would often be postings for work. I spotted a posting where help was needed to pick strawberries and a bus would pick anyone interested up, on Saturday morning at 7:00 AM. Without consulting anyone I jumped at it. I should have noticed there may be a problem when I got on the bus and found that I was the only person with pale skin. This fact went over my head and I was basically ignored by everyone until I got to the farm where we were to pick strawberries. Fortunately, there was one rather large but very kind woman who took me aside and asked me a few questions. When she realized that I knew absolutely nothing about picking, she taught me a few of the ropes. Where the baskets were, how you picked the fruit, how you piled them in each quart container so as not to damage them and how you kept track of yours so you could get paid. I struggled. It was tough work and you had to know what you were doing and be efficient at it. I did not make much money that day but the main lesson for the day was yet to come. When my Aunt Virginia learned of my working with the "poor" people, she was not happy about my entrepreneurial spirit. Our family did not realize it, but we were soon to learn that it was not a proper thing to mix with the "coloreds," and I in particular better not do it again.

Summer was interesting in Ft. Smith to say the least. Perhaps my Aunt Virginia had a problem with associating with the "coloreds" but I had no such apprehensions. I had one friend whose last name was "Ingram." Perhaps it was insensitive but only out of ignorance and not malice that he went by the name of "Inke" with some calling him "Ink Spot." I never associated it with the color of his skin; however, looking back I can see how this was ignorant of me to not make the connection. But Inke was a good chum. We picked "Polk (Poke) Salad" for the Highway 22 store. There was pretty good money in it and we were always trying to make some money. They only sold Polk Salad greens in the early spring as they were said to become poisonous when they matured. They boiled and drained the greens several times before frying them in oil. I ate it once fried in bacon fat and then mixed with black eyed peas. I believe it was a remnant of the hard times when any food was appreciated. I would not say I would eat it again.

*The Herman Druyvesteyn Family*
*top; H.J. Humpy, Frank, Tom - middle; Etta, Agness - bottom; Adrian, Jennie, Herman*

*1969 Tom Druyvestein Family*
*top; Mike, Yvonne, Don, Karen, Terry - bottom; Gin, Ione, Tom, Donna*

Things did not work out well for my dad working for his brother. Humpy found the best equipment mechanic in the world in my dad and wanted Tom to maintain his equipment and not compete against him for excavation jobs. It was soon realized that his working with his brother in the contracting business was not going to work out. That coupled with a bunch of unhappy kids wanting to go back to South Dakota where they had friends, convinced my dad to pack up and after exactly one year, we returned to Lake Andes. We all cheered all the way back home. Like when we moved down, we travelled back with my father driving the truck mounted backhoe, me driving the panel welding truck full of clothes and personal goods and my mother driving the family car filled with five of the kids. We did not stop at restaurants or motels. We camped out and ate from grocery bags. That is just the way we saved money for gas. In Missouri, without gas taxes, we bought gas for $0.18 per gallon. No need to say this but a dollar was worth a lot more in those days but they also were harder to come by.

We left in September and Humpy came down for pheasant hunting in October. I do not know if my dad and Humpy had disagreements over their separation, but if they did they did not let it be known to the rest of us. As far as I was concerned and as far as I knew, they were brothers and still were the best of friends. Humpy came hunting pheasants and when we moved to the Black Hills in western South Dakota in 1958 Humpy would come each fall for the deer hunting.

One thing I loved but at the time probably did not appreciate enough, was the closeness we had as a family – we were poor but we certainly did stick together. We all would come home for Christmas – we all would rekindle our relationship and catch up on what was happening in each others' lives – we all were interested in each other's kids. We played Monopoly and trivia games and my four sisters would keep us in stitches with their unique sense of humor. Our mother gave that to them as she was always "right in there" with them – but us boys, although light hearted in many ways, could never match their wit. I would come home twice a year but in particular I would never miss Christmas. It was not until my two sons were in high school that

I finally missed a Christmas with my siblings. My boys got involved so heavily in their own lives that they had to pass on traveling to South Dakota at Christmas. This is the way it should be I guess.

So this is the way it went until December of 1970 when my dad died. My dad never went to the doctors. "We never had the money," he would say and he was tough, no doubt about that. But tough is not enough when you have an attack from cancer. My dad knew there was a serious problem when he had pains in his gut and started passing a lot of blood. Being a veteran and having a Veterans Hospital in Hot Springs, just 21 miles south of us, he finally consented to get things checked out. They operated on him for colon cancer but it did not look good. The cancer had spread to his liver and back then, they did not operate on the liver. I was living in Missoula, Montana and as I mentioned, I usually came back home twice a year. So when Dad got near to the end I came home to help my mother with his care. Dad wanted to be at home and not in the hospital. I was home in December and I would give Dad shots of pain killers about every four hours. I recall him grimacing in pain and asking me to give him a shot. I would look at my watch and if it was not yet four hours I would say so and would not give him one. My dad would then say, "Oh, OK, I can wait." I look back now and see how stupid I was. Now, with severe pain, doctors allow shots whenever people need them. Have you ever done things you wish you could change? I have to say that for me this was one of those things.

Not long before Christmas, I told Mom that I needed to go back to Missoula and get my family and we would then come back for Christmas. I wanted to know if she would be OK until I got back. What a stupid question! She hated to give the shots. I did too, for that matter. We would give them in the arm and the muscle tissue would get tough as leather. It often would be very hard to drive the needle in. She said she would try to manage but she was almost at the end of her ability, and looking back there were not many other choices available to us.

Before I left, I went into my dad's room and talked with him. It is funny how, having lived in the same house for much of our lives, that now we were having a truly heart to heart talk. My dad was just 52 and

I was 29 years old. I asked if we could pray before I left. He said that would be good. Dad was brought up in a strong Christian home and had tried to remain faithful through his years. He fell away when we were still living on the lake near Lake Andes as a result of being visited by the elders of the church. They had heard that we had been "selling bait" and "renting boats" on Sundays. The fact was that Sundays were our biggest days. Well, it seems that we were contributing to the fall of others who would go fishing rather than go to church on Sundays. If he was to remain a church member in good standing, we would have to close up shop on Sundays. The fact that most of the elders were farmers and "had" to work on Sundays when the crops were ready to harvest made no difference to them. When the Lord ripened the crops they had to be harvested, Sunday or whatever. Our business was not the same and should not be open. Dad, on the other hand, and primarily my mom, saw to it that us kids went to church and got confirmed in the faith. So, when my dad agreed to pray with me it was the first time in my life that we had done so together. It also was the first time that my dad acknowledged that he would soon die. He had always tried to be strong and told us that he "would beat this cancer" one way or the other. He now confided that he was losing the battle, so we prayed that he would make it till Christmas so that he could see all of his family one more time. The last thing he said before we separated was, "Terry, take care of your mom and the kids." (meaning in particular my youngest sister, still living at home) Those would be words I would remember and try to live up to.

I went back to Missoula and was getting things in order at work and home so we could travel back to the Black Hills when I got the call that Dad had passed away. Mom did her best but soon after I left, Dad realized it was too much for her to care for him and he asked to go back to the Veteran's Hospital. He was admitted that day and passed that night just four days before Christmas.

When I got back to our ranch near Pringle, South Dakota, my uncle Humpy had heard the news and had come immediately all the way from Ft. Smith, Arkansas. Funeral arrangements had been made and my dad was laid to rest just a mile from our home in the Pringle Cemetery. There is a community church in Pringle and my mom had always been fairly active going there. Dad had gone there also but was not really active. After the graveside service was over a pastor came over by my side and said he was from the V. A. Hospital. He was a chaplain there and wanted to tell me he was blessed to have known my father. He explained that he had been struggling with his faith when he met my father and his talks with Dad had done more to get him through those times and strengthen his faith than anything else. That testimony helped me a lot.

When Humpy left to return to Arkansas after having spent a couple days with our family, he said, "Terry, if there is anything you need you just call me, OK?" Humpy had become quite wealthy in the past years and he offered a hand to help out. Humpy struggled with periodic alcoholic binges and my Dad went to Arkansas whenever he was called to get Humpy out of the bars and back on track. Dad had struggled himself with alcohol addiction and had trouble keeping his head above water financially. I knew my dad had very little cash but he had a small ranch of 69 acres which he said was clear of debt, and he had a few cows. He had bought some excavation equipment, the financial status of which I had no idea.

Christmas was a sad and hard one, yet all of the family felt joy that the suffering was over and that Dad was now in the hands of Christ, who he had trusted in. I decided I needed to check into the equipment loan which dad had with a used equipment dealer and financier in Rapid City. Mom would not be able to handle these financial details after I left so it was best to get them straightened out now. Mom had records of the purchase of a used back hoe and a front end loader. The initial price was around $7,000 and payments had been made for over a year before Dad came down with cancer. The balance had been down to a little over $5,000 when Dad had become too ill to continue. I wondered to myself, if they could take the equipment back for the amount which was owed on it? I thought it was a straight forward path that we must take. We must first pay this loan off, secure some kind of financial help from those of us siblings who could afford to do so and finally make it

11

possible for our mother to recover from the untimely loss of our father. He was after all, only 52 years old when he died and my mother, the same age, had a lot of life yet to live. It is odd, and not complimentary how, as a young man of 29, I did not fully recognize just how young my mother was. I never thought of how she could or even should remarry. Looking back now, from the age of 79, I can see that those thoughts were not only naïve, but pretty immature.

I came to realize what Dad was saying when he said "take care of your mom and kids." He was worried primarily about my mom but he was also worried about those still at home and especially Ginny who was only 16. This was coming home to me now. It was a blessing that they lived on a small ranch, had a garden, and plentiful wood supply and though it was not much, they had a house. They would have everything they needed to live if we could get them a little spending money for clothes, some food, electricity etc. I had one older sister who was just married and perhaps not in a financial position to help, at least not quite yet. I had an older brother who had just graduated with a teaching degree and just a few months earlier went to Alaska with his wife and had not yet had time to put away much, if any, savings. I had one younger sister who might help but she was just getting started herself. I had a younger brother who was trying to go to college and was only 19. I was sure they would all help and rally around the care for our mother and little sister. So all I needed to do was pay off the loan and even if the equipment could not be sold for what was now owed on it, there could not be much debt and I was well established, having worked for six years out of college and had savings in the bank. We would make this work just fine. I was in for the shock of my life.

The balance against the equipment loan was now $19,561. As the story went, the equipment company had mercifully come down to visit Dad soon after he had come down with cancer and was unable to make payments. They told my dad, "Tommy, don't worry yourself about those payments." As good friends of his, they would take care of it for him until he got back on his feet. They had Tom and Ione both sign the papers which would now allow them to carry the loan until he was well again. Mom and Dad had signed. I asked Mom if she knew what she had signed and if they had explained it to her? She said, "Dad signed, so I just signed where they asked me to." I asked if she had known that she was signing over her home. She said that she "simply did not do that, nor did Dad." Dad had told her "There were no mortgages against the home place." She was convinced she never signed papers against the ranch property.

I have a good friend, who is savvy in the investment world and especially in land contracts, who has told me that the thing you must always remember when dealing in these type of contracts is that "your banker is not your friend." We have a tendency to regard the people who are loaning us money, for our house, land or whatever, as our friends and that they are looking out for our best interests. They may act like that, but they are not, remember that! They are in the business of making money for their investors, not making things easier for you. But even with that knowledge, how could one even fathom that a debt of $5,000 remaining on a loan for some equipment, could turn into a $19,561 obligation against your home in just a little over two years? It was preposterous! It must be illegal and there must be something we could do to right this wrong.

I went to see a lawyer in Custer just 12 miles north of our place in the small town where I had graduated from high school in 1959, 11 years before. I did not know any lawyers but my sister Donna, who then lived in Custer and worked in the courthouse, was able to give me the name of a woman lawyer who seemed to be well respected for her ability and compassion with helping people who were being "screwed" by the finance companies. Flora was a good woman but had bad news. What the equipment company had done was put a "new contract in place," making it possible to change their interest rate and remake the loan every month. Every month they would add past interest due, refinance charges and of course a penalty. Compound every month for about two years and you have a $5,000 debt grow to almost four times, or to $19,561.

There is no question that what this company did was take advantage of unsuspecting people, at least that would seem to be the case based on our inherent sense of fairness. Why then could they get away with doing it? Because it was legal to do so, and they did. Regardless of how my parents may have been hurt, or even if they were taken advantage of, what they took was legal and in their minds "just good business." South Dakota did not have any usury laws preventing finance companies from charging outlandish rates, and more importantly allowing them to shrewdly attach our mother's home to insure that they would get their money or would happily take our ranch. They had the signatures of our dad and our mother and nobody could say that they had coerced them into signing their names to the documents. Perhaps there is a time when you yourself have been short of cash and had to borrow, no matter the cost. In the military or on construction jobs, young people in particular often get over extended and short of cash, so they borrow from a loan shark, often at "two will get you one." Well these cases are in themselves, at the very least, "high risk" loans and one can justify a high interest rate but the ethics of taking such an advantage of your fellow man is hard to accept. In my parents' case however, I have to wonder at such a high interest rate on a well secured loan. First, the loan was secured by the full value of the equipment which the original loan was made on, so why was it necessary to re-secure it with their house and land? The only thing that I can conclude is that the penalties, refinancing charges and new interest rates which would now be used justified more collateral to secure the loan. It would be like owing on your car and refinancing it by using your home as collateral. I guess you need to make up your mind on the fairness of this one.

South Dakota to this day does not have a usury law with respect to the maximum amount of interest a financial institution can charge for a loan. So this is a situation where, since there was not a law preventing it, the finance company considered it legal to do whatever they wanted. Just because something does not have a law preventing an action, do we lose our sense of fairness and something that is deemed to be legal then becomes something acceptable? There should be, and I am certain there used to be, a general law of fairness and equitability. The absence of a specific law should not preempt the general law of "fair and equitable", or even the oldest of laws "thou shalt not steal." We should not need a specific numbers law when something is so far from what is reasonable that we lose all sense of fairness. I really wonder how many poor people find themselves in this type of situation. It makes me feel for them.

To put things in perspective, I was then living in a new home in Missoula, Montana. It was in a good neighborhood, three bedrooms, full basement, and it had cost me $19,500 which was about what was now owed against my mother's place. Our mother's house was very small and old, but it rested on a small 69-acre homestead surrounded by forest land. It was a private location and it was her home. It was worth fighting for and even though the house was run down, it was all Mom had. I tried to get a loan against the property but no one would loan that much money on just the raw land, they considered the house a liability and not a valuable asset. I thought about Humpy and his offer, "Terry, if there is anything you need, just call me." Surely he could help me with a loan.

With all other avenues shut, I called Humpy. I told him that I thought I could sell the equipment back to the equipment dealer for I hoped, about $5,000 or what had been owed against it when Dad came down with cancer. I could muster up about $4,000 in cash and savings and could he loan me about $10,500 or maybe $11,000? He talked to his wife Bobbie about it and she flatly said no. They had loaned a lot of money out to her son and they were in no position to loan more. Humpy had divorced his first wife Virginia, or rather I should say that she had divorced him and took the construction company which he had started and run for most of his life. Humpy received their land holdings and apartment buildings in the settlement. He had then married Bobbie, this being his second wife. She controlled the purse strings for Humpy. Anyway, Humpy said that their assets were all tied up at the time, but that he could look for someone who might be willing to loan me the money against the land. With Humpy being in Arkansas and me needing money in South Dakota, I thought there was not much of a chance for that, at least not on any reasonable financing terms.

# CHAPTER TWO

## The Uncle

When we finished with greetings on the tarmac at Ft. Smith in April of 1999, those present were Humpy, my wife Loretta and me. Humpy's wife Bobbie was home in bed and not feeling that well. In fact, it seemed that she had been like that a lot recently and Humpy had to stay near home. Bobbie would call for Humpy to get something and Humpy would be right on it. I was impressed with the attention he gave her and if ever there was a devoted husband, it was Humpy in his care of Bobbie. It is great to see devotion from a spouse when their partner in life becomes incapacitated. Whether it is a result of injury or diminished cognitive function, it takes a devoted spouse to stick with the full time job often needed to keep the spouse at home. On the other hand, there is a limit as to what sometimes can be done and I appreciate that also.

It was apparent that Humpy also needed a break. I have been around a number of couples who were very much devoted to each other, especially in the final years of life. My mother, regardless of the fact that my father was in many ways a less than ideal spouse, was devoted to my father till the end. It seems that we have a great capacity to forgive those who wish to be forgiven. It also seems much harder to forgive those who do not even recognize that they should ask for forgiveness. Whatever the reasons, Humpy was dedicated to Bobbie but when we were there, Loretta, being a retired RN, would be counted on to give Bobbie the attention which she required at least for a half day at a time. Humpy had invited me down to "do a little crappie fishing." We had kept in touch over the years, and even though Humpy had asked me many times to come down to Arkansas and fish with him, I had never before taken him up on the offer. I had decided to restore the close relationship we had before my father had passed away and a good step in that direction would be to go down and do some fishing together.

Humpy lived in Barling, Arkansas. I had remembered the town as being very small in 1955 when our family had lived there for a year, but now it was much larger. As a suburb of Ft. Smith, Barling had grown and Humpy had recently constructed a new house with a guest house in the back. It was a perfect place for Loretta and me to stay while Humpy and I would catch up on old times. Humpy was wearing his DJ&A cap which I had sent him several years before. The names for the logo were spelled out above it as Druyvestein, Johnson & Anderson and below the logo the inscription "Engineers and Surveyors." Humpy was happy to have me, his nephew, represent his name in the construction industry he had worked in all of his life. Over the coming week Humpy would take us around to the places where his construction shops had been located. He also showed us where my dad and mom had lived with the seven kids of our family in 1955. All of the housing had changed with new houses and businesses taking the place of the much smaller houses of the era I was remembering. Of course he also took us to his favorite crappie fishing lakes.

We would fish Tenkiller Ferry Lake where Humpy had a cabin when I had lived there before. More commonly called Lake Tenkiller, it is a reservoir on the Illinois River located in eastern Oklahoma. It was constructed between 1947 and 1952 so when our family was in Ft. Smith in 1955, Tenkiller was a hot fishing spot. Humpy still liked to go there. We had a great time. I had not fished for crappies in a long time, not since our family moved from Lake Andes in eastern South Dakota to Pringle in the Black Hills of western South Dakota. Humpy loved to fish from his small boat, use a long bamboo pole and drop his bobber and minnow over a log or other type of cover into a "hole" where the crappie would spot it drifting down and come out of the cover to take the bait. You needed to hook the minnow, about a 1½ incher, through just under the skin in the tail, so it would continue to wiggle. As I remember, we had some pretty good catches of fish, but the main thing is that we were getting together as family again. Fishing is a great time to tell stories and catch up on life. We were not so intent on catching crappies that we had to be really quiet. Humpy told me about his best friends who he always fished with. One was a retired highway patrolman and the other was a regular guy named Hub. Their common bond revolved around fishing but their friendship was mutual and ran deep. He had quit his "drinking days" many years ago and had even spent quite a few years teaching Sunday school at his church. He was still active in his church and went regularly. We talked about our family, about my dad having cancer, and touched upon what our family did to pull together after Dad had died. I could tell he felt bad about not helping us during this time; however I tried to assure him that we had got along fine. Mom was doing well, still lived on the home place. My mom was happy and had a new house. Our family, basically all of the siblings, had come back home in the summer of 1980 and built my mom a new, two bedroom, one bath, basic home with a two car attached garage. She had never had a new home and it brought her much joy. I am certain us siblings were given as much or more joy in working together for a little over a month, 12 hours and more per day, to make this dream house come true. We would work hard all day, including three of our teenaged sons, and visit and eat big family meals at night. To this day, this is perhaps the most satisfying accomplishment that I worked on with all of my family.

I explained to Humpy what had happened after he was "unable" to loan us the money to keep the house and ranch together when my dad had died. Facing the foreclosure of the equipment loan, I was able to get the equipment company to take the backhoe and front end loader back for what was owed against them when Dad got sick. That basically left a balance of $14,500 owing against the home place. In other words, that was the amount the financer had charged for penalties and interest for the two years my dad had quit making payments. Flora, our lawyer, was able to get a third party to loan us $7,000 against the land. I had about $2,500 in cash and savings and was able to get a second mortgage against my house and car for the remaining $5,000. That's about all there was to it.

It seems that when we as humans have a big challenge ahead of us that we can come together and meet the challenge. When things are too easy we become complacent and demanding and cannot meet the challenges of even the simplest of tasks. I thank my older brother Don for offering to handle half of the note payments. I don't believe I could have handled that, but he and his wife, just out of school and teaching in a village in Alaska, stepped up to the plate and made it possible. So that's how we did it. A big family has advantages. All of my siblings would step up in the next years to help my mother and youngest sister, especially helping them with living expenses and the necessities of life. Perhaps things were very tough in the first several years for Mom and her youngest, Ginny, but as time passed and finances improved, things got better because of the love this big family had for each other.

I look back at my dad going into WWII when he was 25 years old with three young children and one about to be born. How could he make the decision to volunteer into the Army? I think he saw his brother Humpy go in, his brother Frank also, and his wife's two brothers go in, so he had to do it also. He had to quit his construction job building military camps, bring his family to Corsica to be with his wife's family and volunteer into the Army. I think Tom Brokaw had it right when he called these people "The Greatest Generation."

As I mentioned earlier, Bobbie was not doing too well health wise. Humpy looked after her hand and foot and Bobbie was a demanding woman. It was good that Loretta and I were staying in the guest house and it was also good that Bobbie's daughter Sue lived across the back yard fence from Humpy's main house. Sue's husband was Bob Rose and he often would tag along with Humpy to the Black Hills to hunt many years earlier with my dad. Bobbie was always concerned that Humpy may give away some of the inheritance money she had deemed was rightfully hers and her daughters. Humpy and his first wife Virginia were not able to have children and when Humpy married Bobbie, they were pushing the years to have their own children also. I think in her final years Bobbie realized that the South Dakota Druyvesteins' need not be considered a threat and started to relax her fears. At the time of my dad's passing, however, Bobbie was instrumental and did what she needed to do by not allowing Humpy to help us with a loan to save the home place. We were not asking for a hand out, we just wanted a loan, perhaps one that was not backed by excessive collateral, but one backed by a family she did not fully trust. I believe Bobbie was very concerned to create a family loan relationship with the South Dakota Druyvesteins, as that could come into conflict with her own family's interests and lead to a closer relationship with blood relatives.

My dad and mom had always treated Humpy and all of his family with respect and hospitality when coming to the Black Hills to hunt. In addition, I think over the years Bobbie had managed to transfer most of their properties into a trust for her family, thus alleviating fears that we were trying to sidetrack their inheritance. Humpy's house and guest house had been willed to her family along with extensive land holdings which had been leased to build a bank and a Lowes Hardware store and a liquor store which Bob and his son Jon now ran. Also some other acreage which Humpy had used to run some cattle on were now prime development acres. The Rose family was now well taken care of and I, for one, was happy for them and had no interest in property which would go to their family. I simply wanted to rebuild my relationship with Humpy.

I had an enjoyable time with Humpy and all too quickly we were to separate and go our own ways again. I offered that Humpy should come to Montana to reciprocate but he was skeptical because of the time it now took to take care of Bobbie. I understood this, but it was something to keep in the back of his mind, that he was welcome, when the time came.

Later that summer, Bobbie did pass away. Humpy called with the news that Bobbie was put to rest and he had bought a cemetery plot for himself to be buried next to her when at some point in the future he would go. Also, he needed to get away and if he wanted, we would like to have him come for a visit. My brother Don would also like to show him some of the fishing out of Juneau, Alaska. Don, who had worked for Humpy when we were in Arkansas in 1955, had gone on for a career in teaching the Inuit people in Bethel, Alaska. Bethel is a fairly remote town on the Kuskoquim River near the west coast of Alaska and the Bering Sea. Don had a son Jay, who was married and had a family he should meet, and was now living in Juneau where he would arrange for a fishing trip. Don was retired in Sequim, Washington so would be available to travel with Humpy to Juneau. This then became the plan: Humpy would fly to Seattle, go with Don to Alaska, do some fishing there, return to his place in Sequim, and then they would travel together to Montana, where I had a cabin on Flathead Lake, and we would fish for some trout. He would fly back to Arkansas from Missoula, where my home was.

Humpy had a great time. The Alaska wilderness was something he had never experienced before. They had gone out on a friend's boat and stayed on the boat several nights, anchored in the wilds of Alaska. If you have never "anchored out" in an inlet such as Icy Straight or Glacier Bay or something similar, you need to put it on your list. Hearing the whales blow, the fish jump at night and look into a sky full of stars, undiminished by background lights, is a treat worth enjoying. They had fished for salmon and halibut and caught some of each. It was a great trip for Humpy and he enjoyed it tremendously.

I was not yet retired but I arranged for the time to be with Humpy when he came to Missoula after his Juneau trip. I wanted him to meet the rest of my family. So far he really only had met my wife, Loretta, and of course he had heard about, but had not met my two sons. My oldest son Paul lived in Missoula and was also a civil engineer and worked in the company I had started. With his wife and three children, we had a nice dinner together. We then went to Polson, which is about 70 miles north of Missoula, on the south end of Flathead Lake, and traveled to the country home where my youngest son Ken lives. There we got into the work of butchering about 20 spring fryers. These are young chickens which are raised entirely for their meat and it brought back memories for Humpy of his younger days before he had left home. He was very excited to catch the chickens, chop off their heads with an ax, and scald them in hot water to loosen the feathers before removing them. This reminded him of good things, survival and growing up, but many young people today and some of you reading this would be horrified with the butchering process.

We then traveled north about 30 miles along the west shore of Flathead Lake to where my cabin is located. Flathead lake is a pristine, clear water lake, which receives the snowmelt from Glacier National Park and the Bob Marshal Wilderness area. Flathead is a huge lake almost 30 miles long and 15 miles across at the longest points. It boasts to be the "largest natural freshwater lake west of the Mississippi River." It is the largest by volume as it is over 300 feet deep, thus beating Devils Lake in North Dakota. It is natural as it is not entirely formed by a dam, thus beating the impounds on the various rivers. It is fresh water, thus beating out the Great Salt Lake in Utah. Just shows one how important adjectives are. It is a cold water lake and the temperature at the surface gets up to only about 70 degrees in August. Humpy enjoyed the unbelievably clear water and the lake trout we caught. We would jig for the trout mostly, in water 100 to 150 feet deep and it was good fishing. We continued to talk about old times. Humpy brought up the issue of my dad drinking too much. It was true, my dad did drink too much, but Humpy should have been the last person to criticize. It was not until Humpy was at least ten years older than the age of my father when he died, that he finally had enough and quit drinking himself. I remember at least three times when my father left his work and family, went to Arkansas as a result of a call from one of his wives, found out where his brother was staying for his drunken spree, got him out of there and "dried him out." I did not take issue with my uncle's statement but I did tell Humpy that his brother did completely quit drinking the last two years of his life and probably felt a lot of remorse for the years he

23

had spent drinking. This was after he had learned of his cancer, which was perhaps too late for his health but not too late for his spirit.

I would come to Arkansas for a visit the next year, in the spring when the crappie fishing was the best. After these visits we decided that we really needed to hold a Druyvesteyn Reunion soon, so Humpy could get reacquainted with all of the family. We would hold the first reunion in the Black Hills where most of my siblings and mother still lived and we would invite all of the families of Humpy's siblings as well. In the Druyvesteyn family there were three sisters and three sons. All offspring of these six would be invited. You may have noticed by now that the last names of Humpy and my father are spelled differently. The last "y" was replaced with a "i" in my family's name. When my father worked construction the social security system came into being. The name was misspelled and instead of going through the trouble of changing it, my dad left it as spelled. With the "stein" ending, many people thought our family was Jewish. Druyvesteyn is Dutch however, and the name goes back many generations to the original man who took the name. Dirk Janszoon Druyvesteyn was born in 1520. The first Druyvesteyn to immigrate to the United States was my grandfather's father, Francois Constantyn Willem Druyvesteyn, who came to Iowa in 1878. There are not many Druyvesteyns and I believe I know all of them that now live.

The first Druyvesteyn reunion would be held on July 20th and 21st of 2002. The reunion would be held at the ranch of my mother Ione Druyvestein in the Black Hills of South Dakota, where Humpy had come many times to hunt whitetail deer with my father Tom, many years ago. There were three of this generation still living but only two could attend the 2002 reunion. Humpy and of course our mother Ione, the wife of Tom, Humpy's older brother. Ann, the wife of Frank, the eldest brother, could not attend. . In all, 40 would attend.

The reunion was not without its surprises. Perhaps the biggest "bombshell" was that Humpy showed up with a new wife! Wife number three was Lois. Humpy had known Lois through the church they both attended and Lois was eager to establish herself as Mrs. Lois Druyvesteyn. She pressed hard to "fit in" but hovered over Humpy perhaps a little more than what was necessary. I personally thought she was OK if she made Humpy happy, even though she was younger than I was. I never was able to exactly determine her age, but then what does age have to do with it when you are in love? My mother, on the other hand did not like her. Lois made the mistake of confiding in Mom about taking showers with Humpy after they were first married and some details of their sex life which Mom really did not want to hear, and she said "this made her sick." It made me smile that Mom did not need these details as she was then 84 and these details were from a much younger woman, a woman she simply considered a "gold digger" in the first place. I shrugged it all off as a consequence of their age difference, although I was a little suspicious of Lois's intentions and quickness of the marriage.

*The Druyvesteyn Family Reunion 2002*

*Bottom row – Humpy, 3rd from left, new wife Lois at his right shoulder and my mother Ione at his left*

*The Druyvestein Family 2002*
*top; Virginia, Terry, Donna and Karen - bottom; Mike, Ione and Don*

After the reunion Humpy seemed to be quite happy. Although not regularly, Humpy and I talked on the phone at least once per month. He wanted me to come to Ft. Smith fishing in 2003 but I had retired the year before and I was planning a trip to Prince of Whales Island in Alaska with Loretta and some long time friends of our family. I just could not make it this year but we would make it up next year as we were planning a second reunion.

I don't remember the exact time of the call. It was sometime in 2003, when Humpy pulled me up short by calling me with an important matter. He said that he wanted me to have a certain Ford Motor Company bond when he passed away. I told him that he should cash it in for himself and he and Lois should travel a little. Come here more often and enjoy life. I asked him about Lois, was she in favor of this. He said that he had taken care of Lois. She had enough of his personal money and that he was also building a couple of duplexes which could be used for their income as they were paid for and there were no mortgage payments. They would be used by Lois in the event that he passed away first. He said that he only wanted the interest from the bond each year to live on and that he was naming me the TOD (Transfer on Death) beneficiary to the bond. He said that he was having his broker, Donna Young, call me and get the details from me to complete the designation. It was his wish that I should have this. He did not say it, but I knew that he still felt bad for not helping me out with the family ranch after my dad had passed away in 1970. It occurred to me that he also recognized what my dad had done to help him through his own alcohol problems. Whatever the case was I will never know, but I accepted and told him that if he did this, and I was thankful to him for it, that I would plan to share it with my mother and all of my siblings. He replied, "I know you will do what is right." That trust in me would mean a lot to me over the following years.

*Humpy and Lois Druyvesteyn*

The Druyvesteyn Family Reunion 2004

2nd row up - Ione 5th from right, Humpy 3rd from right, Ann 2nd from right, Lois far right

As promised, Humpy's financial advisor eventually did call me and got my personal data to make the TOD out. I was designated the TOD for account No. 2895-8136. The bond had a face value of $200,000. I knew this money would mean a lot to our family, especially to my mother, but I said nothing to them. I have been around the block enough times that I did not wish to influence them in their relationship to Humpy and also I know that things can change and people can change their minds. It would be best to wait for a more opportune time and besides Humpy was healthy and perhaps would need the bond in the future to take care of other things in his life.

The second reunion would be held later on July 9th, 10th and 11th of 2004. This reunion would also be held in the Black Hills but this time at the State Park Shelter on Stockade Lake east of Custer, South Dakota. This location would not be far from Ione's ranch where the first reunion was hosted, and it had the advantage of using a shelter in the event a rainstorm would appear at an inopportune time. The second reunion would be a little larger than the first. We would have the family of Arnout Jan Druyvesteyn from the Netherlands in attendance and he would be able to give us more information on the family history. There would be about 55 at this affair. Four generations were represented and the location and weather were excellent. The older generations enjoyed their time to reminisce and the younger generations got to know each other by participating in activities and capturing their memories which they in their future years would use to reminisce with each other.

# CHAPTER THREE

## The New Wife

Humpy had introduced his new wife Lois at the 2002 reunion. Our family had found that the two or three days for that reunion were not enough to really get to know her. There were suspicions of "gold digging" and because of their apparent age difference, about whether she could, in fact, continue to make Humpy happy and care for him in his aging years. Now two years had passed, so at the 2004 reunion we were all anxious to see how things were working out. As it now had been surmised, Lois was somewhere in her mid 60s, at least 15 and most likely close to 20 years younger than Humpy. According to Humpy however, she "was fun to be with" and if she made Humpy happy, we certainly should all be for it. Lois was friendly but curiously much more cautious not to let Humpy out of her sight. At the reunion I thought that Lois was just attentive to Humpy but when, on occasion, he would be annoyed by her hovering over him, I wondered if there was more to it. Lois was never out of ear shot of what Humpy was saying and she often would barge into a conversation so she would not miss anything that was being said. It was hard, if not impossible, to get a somewhat private talk with Humpy. It was because of this difficulty, of being unable to have a good talk with Humpy, that my sisters Donna and Karen went to see Lois and Humpy at their motel the last evening of the reunion. They wanted this one last chance to have a good visit before Humpy and Lois left the next morning to return to their home in Arkansas. After all, they were quite close and knew Humpy very well in their younger years and it felt "empty", as if they never really got to visit with him. Lois met them outside the motel door and said that Humpy was not available. They were turned away by Lois and Humpy did not intervene. Lois said that he was sleeping and that they had a long drive ahead the next day. What could they do? They were certain Humpy would love to talk to them, and it was not at all too late, but to barge past Lois and wake Humpy up, if in fact he was sleeping, would not be acceptable.

The summer passed and winter also. We kept in touch and Humpy seemed to be happy enough. His hearing was failing badly and we had some difficulty having a decent conversation on the phone. I decided that I should go to Arkansas the next summer. My urgency for a visit was hastened by phone calls I was getting from the Bob and Sue Rose families. They had nothing good to say about Lois. She was controlling Humpy and not allowing even his old friends to visit. Humpy was having some health issues and they were not even allowed to see him. They lived just over the fence and hardly ever saw Humpy. In the spring of 2006 Loretta and I made the trip. We decided to drive and to use an extended vacation to see some of Loretta's relatives who also lived in Arkansas, but closer to Little Rock.

When we arrived in Ft. Smith things appeared to be good enough on first entry. We asked about the Rose family and how they were doing. Humpy said good and Lois said nothing. We said that while we were there, perhaps we could get Jon, Bob and Sue's son, to barbeque some of those ribs he had done for us when we were in Barling the last time. Humpy said, great idea, and that why don't we just go over and ask him? Lois was not happy with this and said that they were too busy with our company to go over to the Roses. Humpy brushed it off and we did walk over and talked to Bob in his garage. He said he was sure Jon would be happy to cook up some ribs and that Jon and the granddaughters especially would like to see us and they also had not seen Humpy in a while. I thought it an excellent plan to get the families together again. It certainly was apparent that Humpy had not been over for awhile and the rumors that Lois was not allowing Humpy to visit his family or his old friends were also true. When the late afternoon came for us to go over I thought perhaps Lois would not come. It may be better, I thought, so we could get to the bottom of what Lois was doing to Humpy. Lois was not going to let Humpy out of her sight. When the time came she was right there, ready to come along. I must say that Lois never said a single word all night. She was not a happy camper and did not approve of Humpy visiting with his past family. Humpy however, was in an extremely good mood. He thoroughly enjoyed his family, his granddaughters and the BBQ ribs Jon had prepared. I thought the evening was quite a success but feared that there may be retributions the next day.

To my surprise Lois was fine at the breakfast table the next morning. We had a nice breakfast and toward the end Humpy wanted to talk about family things. He took me around and said that the framed original marriage license of his mom and dad was important to him and he would like me to have it, to keep it in the family. He had given copies of this to all of my siblings and perhaps others of his family but he wanted me to have the original keepsake which was in a frame and hung on their bedroom wall. He also wanted me to have the wood and leather chair that was his dad's and which he now used every morning when seated at the breakfast table. This chair was a place of honor and I still remembered how my grandfather always sat in it, at the head of the table, and no one disrespected his position. These were two family treasures that he had not mentioned to me before and I said that I was honored to have him pass these things along through me for the Druyvesteyn family. He also brought up that he wanted me to have his 12 gauge, Winchester model 12 shotgun that he had always brought to South Dakota hunting pheasants. He had bought it when he was discharged from the army after WWII. He had told me this before but I was happy to have it repeated in front of Lois so there would be no confusion. When Humpy was at my cabin on Flathead Lake he had admired the four guns which hang over my fireplace. At the top is my father's Winchester model 12 shotgun, then Loretta's father's Belgian double barrel shotgun, then Loretta's uncle's .22 caliber rifle, and at the bottom is my brother Don's .22 Winchester Mod. 94 rifle. Now these would be accompanied by Humpy's model 12 Winchester shotgun. Then, he brought up the Ford Motor Company bond and how he had made me the TOD (transfer on death) beneficiary of the bond. I repeated to him, that my family would be very happy to receive this gift and that, as I had told him before, "I would share it with my mother and my brothers and sisters." He repeated, "I know you will do the right thing." I was proud of the fact that he put this kind of trust in me. He never said what the right thing was, but I told him what I thought it should be before and that still was a good plan now.

After the above conversation took place, Humpy excused himself to go to the bathroom. When he was out of the room Lois said to me "You can also thank me for these things, especially the bonds." I said, "Well yes Lois, I also am thankful to you." She said that the Roses were trying to get that money and that she had saved it from them. About that time Humpy returned to the room and nothing more was said about this matter.

I had noticed that in the afternoons Humpy would have a beer or two. He had never drunk when we had visited in the past. I asked Humpy about it and he said he only had one or two a day and Lois picked them up for him at the store. I did not say anything because Humpy was after all, 85 years old and would make up his mind on these things anyway. I do not believe one can tell an alcoholic that he or she should not drink because they know better than anyone else, the dangers in that thinking. What I did not understand is why Lois would participate, even encourage this to happen. I would try to talk to her.

The next day Humpy and Lois took Loretta and me for a long drive. Humpy may have been 85, but he was still an excellent driver. He also knew his way around the town and area he had worked in most of his life. We went to Camp Chaffee where he and my dad Tom had worked. Also my Uncle Henry or "Doc" Vander Pol whose wife was married to my mom's sister, Ruth. We had lived next to each other as we both had travel trailers and that is how we traveled and lived. Humpy did not live with us in the travel trailer camp as he was still single and lived in some bunk houses, or somewhere else, I do not know. We also went past the Lowes Hardware Store where they leased their land from Humpy. Humpy also still owned and leased land to the bank and for the liquor store that Jon Rose now ran. We also went by some land which Humpy pointed out that he still owned and in the recent past had raised a few cattle on. Finally, we came to the cemetery where Bobbie had been buried. Here was the tombstone where his name had already been engraved and where he would be buried next to Bobbie. All that needed to be done was to engrave the date of passing. This was his plan, the cemetery lot was paid for and Lois said that she had the same plan. We then went to a cemetery where Lois's husband was buried. It was here, Lois said, where she would be buried next to him when she passed. These things were all in order.

Through the fall and early winter, it became harder and harder to talk with Humpy. First it was hard when I did get him on the phone because of his hard of hearing issue. I tried to get him to get good hearing aids, but he always passed it off. He had "tried one, once, and it didn't seem to work much." I tried to convince him to go to a hearing specialist and get two, not one aid, and to wear them all of the time. Humpy had a streak of stubbornness and also a streak of frugality, which I think he inherited from his mother. My grandmother was so very "tight" that my dad would say she could squeeze more out of a penny than anyone he knew. I think it was true of the people who went though the Great Depression years. They were frugal. There were things which happened that they would never forget which made them that way. Now we are having the Covid-19 epidemic. It will leave its own special scars on the people who go through it.

The other problem in talking to Humpy was to get past Lois. Lois would often not allow me to talk to him by saying that he was not feeling well or would make an excuse as to why I could not talk to him. I knew it was an attempt not to let us talk as when he was in the room with Lois talking to me on the phone, I could hear Humpy in the background questioning her as to who was calling.

When I could not get through I would call the Rose family, who I explained earlier, lived over the back yard fence. Being Humpy's previous family, they surely would know what was going on with him. They were generally upset that Lois was controlling everything. They would not be allowed to see Humpy; their family, including Humpy's two granddaughters, was not allowed to visit. They even said that Lois was preventing Humpy's old friends from seeing him. Since I had met one of Humpy's old friends on a previous trip, I wrote to him. Hub was perhaps the last of Humpy's really close friends, so I asked him what was going on. Hub was not well versed in a lot of things but he was by all accounts a

> "This is old Hub. First of all I can't speel hardely any thing so mabe you can make out what I try to speel. Humpy liked to talk about his work. When he was younger, we had some good times togather. We fished quite a bit and rode four-wheelers. But that all stopped when he married Lois. She never wanted Humpy to be with any one if she was not there to hear what was sead. We got to go driving a round maybe two or three times after she got Humpy. We would drive down to the lake. Just looking a round. Humpy liked that. But, Lois never liked for us to do that. I wanted to tell Humpy what she was after, but he would never belived me and it would only hurt his feelings. She was pretty slick at what she was doing. Any way, I sure wish I knew some thing to help you. I am pretty sure she has Humpy where he would do what she sead. Probely if he sead anything she would never do what it was."

By all accounts, it appeared that Humpy was being held captive in his own home, by a younger and stronger person and not allowed to have any contact with his former life. I felt sick about this but was not sure there was anything I could do. I may be his blood relative, but Lois was his lawfully wedded wife. The Rose family also had little authority as they were simply the family of a woman, Bobbie, who was the second wife of Humpy and she was now deceased. I got the message from the Roses that they felt Lois was trying to "kill" Humpy. Perhaps not directly, but by how she was pushing alcohol on him and not caring for him properly. They said that Humpy had been in the hospital recently and Lois had left strict instructions that no one was to be allowed to visit except her or specific people to whom she had given her written approval. Not anyone else! Also he was to have no phone nor could he receive any phone calls. Humpy was in the hospital for a little over two weeks, but was then discharged and allowed to go home. I called Humpy several times and got no answer. Finally, I did get Lois on the line and she allowed me to talk to Humpy. Our conversation was difficult. Humpy, not clearly hearing what I said, and me, not having the freedom to ask the questions I really wanted to ask, left me with a feeling of emptiness. I knew Lois was closely listening as she would sometimes repeat the question to Humpy and then he would answer. I wondered if Humpy was very coherent and if he was confused with a multitude of drugs he was probably taking. I also wondered if he was getting any alcohol after he returned home. It did not take things long to deteriorate further. In the winter of 2007, Humpy was admitted to the hospital several times. The scenario continued. I would get my information mostly from the Rose family, who were certain that Lois was out to terminate Humpy as soon as possible. She was refusing treatments for him, they were not allowed to see him, and the doctors were not allowed to share information about him, they were livid with their inability to do anything about it. On occasion I would get through and talk to Lois, and she would say Humpy was sick but never explained exactly with what, that he was getting the best treatment possible and the Roses were continually giving her a hard time and that she needed to keep them away.

*The Rose Family*
*top; Jon, Alex, Bob - bottom; Irene, Humpy, Sue*

# CHAPTER FOUR

## The Passing

Humpy passed away at the Legacy Health Nursing Home on February 24, 2007. He would have been 86 in March. The cause of death was listed as congestive heart failure. He had not been allowed visitors. I do not know how many days Humpy had been in the nursing home. It could not have been many but this information was not given out. I did not even know that he had even been transferred to the nursing facility. I was informed of Humpy's passing from the Rose family. They had read it in the obituaries. I thought about this, the family which was closest to Humpy for most of his life was excluded from visiting and enjoying his company in his final days, all because of a selfish and controlling wife who entered his life in the last several years. Lois did not even have the decency to let anyone in Humpy's past family know of his passing and worse yet did not let his friends and family know of his whereabouts so they could visit.

I called Lois and to my amazement made a quick contact. I expressed my sorrow over the loss of Humpy and asked how she was doing. I said that I could make reservations and be down there for the funeral. She informed me that they, meaning she, had decided to have a simple funeral for only her close family and it would not be open to others. It was plain that included me. I asked for the name of the funeral home and after receiving it we hung up. What else could be done? The

Druyvestein family was not welcome and neither was the Rose family. I had a feeling of sadness when thinking that Humpy would not have his granddaughters present at his funeral. They would not have the gathering which would center around the celebration of a life so meaningful to them. I also was saddened when realizing that none of his past family nor friends, such as his good friend Hub, had been allowed to visit him in his final days and now would not even be allowed at his funeral. I thought of Humpy and how isolated and alone he must have been in his final days. In actuality there really would not be a funeral, just a burial. How selfish Lois had been in controlling Humpy's final days and wishes. How selfish would she continue to be in the days ahead?

I called a flower shop and ordered that a wreath be sent to the funeral home where Herman John Druyvesteyn was being held for burial. I then called all of my siblings with the message that Humpy had passed away and that I had sent a wreath of flowers on behalf of the Druyvestein family. I also told them none of us would be welcome to attend the funeral per Lois Druyvesteyn's wishes. All were disappointed in Lois's behavior but not surprised.

None of the actions of Lois set well with me and I waited a couple of weeks before contacting her again. In the meantime I was getting feedback from Sue Rose, who lived just across the fence from Humpy's home, which now would be passed on to the Rose family, but where Lois was still residing. It turned out that they were not allowed to attend the funeral and were livid when they learned that Lois went against the wishes of Humpy and the Rose family and instead had Humpy buried in her cemetery with her former husband leaving a space between them for her in the future. This was contrary to that which was made perfectly clear to Loretta and I when we had visited less than a year before. Humpy was to be buried with his previous wife Bobbie, and Lois would be buried with her previous husband. It seems that nothing was sacred with Lois so I needed to talk to her. It took a few calls but I finally got Lois on the line. Fortunately, she still would take my calls and regarded me actually as an ally in her fight with the Rose family. The first thing out of her mouth was, "Did you get your money yet?"

She was referring to the bond that Humpy had left our family. I said that "No, I have not yet looked into that." She told me to get it right away as Jon Rose was after her money and would be after mine also. So to me it was plain, Lois was most interested in Humpy's money and not interested in Humpy, his family nor his friends. I was not concerned with Jon but would soon find out I should be more concerned about Lois. What I had called about was the conversation which we had last May when visiting and Humpy's directions with respect to his and her burial wishes and for the personal items such as the family clock, grandpa's special chair, Humpy's shotgun and the wedding certificate for Humpy's mother and father, my grandparents. Lois said that she and Humpy had made additional plans for their burials and essentially that this was not my concern. Lois did not remember instructions for the shotgun, but if that was Humpy's wish, I could have that. I asked Lois to set them aside from her belongings which she was removing from the house. She had thirty days to vacate Humpy's home and she was pissed off about it. The will which Humpy left, allowed Lois thirty days to live in the house. It had been willed to the Rose family along with the guest house and a number of other things. I thought it ironic that Lois would be pissed off about that and not even acknowledge the pain she had caused the Rose family by cutting them off from Humpy, burying him, not with their mother, but with her past husband! When she gained control, Lois had not allowed them to be even a small part of Humpy's life. Anyway, Lois said that she did not want to set our family items aside. She would take care of them and ship them to me when she moved out. I felt uncomfortable with this arrangement but could only hope that Lois would follow through.

I decided to check with Humpy's financial advisor as Lois was a loose cannon and I was not certain whom I should believe about something as large as a $200,000 bond. I called Donna Young and inquired about the bond. She said that everything was in order and it appeared that our best approach would be to first get her a copy of the death certificate, and then we could set up a new account just for holding the bond monies until we could distribute them. She also wanted me to provide to her a list of names of my siblings so that we could distribute the funds directly to each one of them and avoid there being any problem with gift taxes should it all go to me first and then out to them. This sounded like a good plan so I readily agreed to get this all done. The bond was now trading well below par however, so we would not get the full value of the bond. In fact, we would lose about 15% if we cashed it in now. On the other hand, the bond had a life insurance rider and if we could wait until April to cash it, we could redeem it at par plus accumulated interest. In either event, she would immediately change the address with Summit Brokerage Services so that a new account, in my name, could be used to start sending the monthly statements and to hold the funds until they would be distributed. Donna said that Lois had already been in and had established her account and wanted to cash her bond in ASAP. I asked if that bond also had a rider on it to guarantee redemption at full value and she affirmed that it had the rider also but that perhaps the anniversary date was different and Lois did not want to wait. I said that our family was not in a hurry to redeem the bond and that we would wait for the next date when we could redeem it at full value, plus accumulated interest. This would be in April and she would make a note to cash it in then and place the funds in the account.

Even with things apparently in order and Lois having already talked to Donna, I still had this nagging feeling that something would go wrong with this plan. For a starter, I did not understand why Donna needed to first get a copy of the death certificate. Since Lois had already cashed her bond in, why did she need another copy of the death certificate? I had the feeling that something was not right with what I was being told. Could someone contest this plan, somehow, some way? This was not a thing that had to be in a will as it was a TOD or "transfer on death" order which was attached only to this bond. It could not therefore, be contested as part of the will. A contest which I felt certainly was going to happen between Lois and the Rose family. I was not that worried that the Rose family would contest our family's bond as my relations with them in the past were certainly good. Along the same path, I did not think Lois had the grounds to contest what was being done. She had full knowledge of what Humpy wanted done with the bond and surely, if she had designs on our family's bond, she would have brought it up with Donna Young when she had set her own account up. I did not know it then, but close to this time, Lois called my sister Karen in South Dakota and asked her if we had gotten our inheritance yet? She told Karen that the Roses were contesting Uncle Humpy's will and the disposition of his assets. She told Karen that the inheritance was large and she was afraid that we would not get our money. She was surprised that we had not discussed it. I would guess that her urgency was in part associated with the fear that something could go wrong with her plans to get as much from Humpy's estate as she could. I do not dismiss the possibility that in the beginning, Lois did love my uncle; however, there is no doubt in my mind looking back on it now, that she was primarily in it for the money and she could not wait any longer to get what she deemed she had coming for having taken care of Humpy for the past four years. She was currently in a lawsuit with the Roses and I believe she was primarily on a fishing expedition to extract any information she could from Karen and also to align allies in the event she needed help in her court case with the Roses which could potentially follow.

I received a call from Sue Rose. Sue told me that they were having problems with getting things settled with Lois. Lois was in effect, looting the house and it was becoming a real pain to get her out. They had to hire a lawyer to keep her from taking things that were attached to the house and did not belong to her. Sue wanted to know if I wanted her to do anything with the personal items which she knew Humpy had wanted my family to have, these being especially his shotgun, grandpa's chair, the framed marriage certificate and the family clock. I told her that Lois had promised to send these items to me when she moved out. Sue said that Lois was at that stage now and in fact had not been around for the past several days. I asked Sue if she would look to see if those items had been set aside or if Lois had taken them and perhaps shipped them to me. It occurred to me that I should mention the bond to Sue as I really did not know for certain how much Humpy had told them about it and if they did not know about it, if they were fine with

43

it. With Lois keeping everything from the Rose family, I was not certain how up to date they were with recent bond changes but since my TOD designation had taken place when Sue was also a TOD, I was fairly confident that they were aware of it. I concluded that I should just let things alone and not invite more problems if the Rose family was not up to date with what Humpy had planned.

Sue looked into the matter with the Druyvesteyn family heirlooms and determined that the marriage certificate was still on the wall and the family clock was there but she could not find the key, and the family chair was still there. She could not find the shotgun but would check into it. They had hired a lawyer to get certain furnishings back from Lois and would find out if she had the shotgun. Lois had a bunch of things, anything not tied down, taken to a storage unit so the shotgun could be there. After a few days Sue called to tell me she had located the shotgun. Lois had given it to their minister at the church where she and Humpy had attended. The minister said that Lois had offered it to him as a gift but quickly said if there was anything wrong with that gifting, he would certainly return it to the estate. He was true to his word and returned it to Sue. The Rose family packed these things up and shipped them to me. When I finally received them I was relieved to have possession of our family keepsakes and to be done dealing with Lois, or so I thought.

March came to an end and we started into April. I figured this would be the month that we cashed in the bond and would be done with the last obstacle to complete the wishes of Humpy and distribute the bond proceeds to my family. I had started to receive the monthly statements from Summit Financial indicating the bond and interest accrued each month. I had also sent Donna Young a list of names with addresses of my siblings so they could receive their distribution when the time came. I called Donna Young and she shocked me when she apologized that she had missed the due date for cashing in the bond at par and that we now would have to wait till October for the next anniversary date. I questioned her as to how she could have missed such an important date and did she not put it on her calendar or even give notice ahead of time that we would be cashing the bond in? She said that it just slipped her mind and if we wanted we could cash it in now. I did not wish to miss the par value nor the interest as I now knew this combined amount would total about $38,000. I had no alternative but to tell her that we would wait until August. I was disgusted with her performance but now I clearly look back and realize that I should have adhered to the advice my friend told me long ago: "Always remember that your banker is not your friend." Not by a long shot, I was soon to learn this lesson for a second time.

So the summer came and was about over. I had received monthly statements on the family account and things were looking positive. I was relieved not to hear anything from Lois nor the Rose family and things seemed to be normal if anything ever is "normal." The interest rate was almost 8% so what could be bad about letting it accumulate for a few more months? That was better than what one could get in a CD or other guaranteed account. What now could possibly go wrong?

On September 9th I received a bombshell in the form of a copy of a letter which was sent from Summit Brokerage Services and was addressed to Lois Druyvesteyn.

August 28, 2007
Lois Druyvesteyn
[REDACTED]

Re: Account of H. J. Druyvesteyn
#2895-8136
Dear Ms. Druyve

With regard to the above-referenced account, the records pertaining to it, including the Application for Registration of Account in Beneficiary Form/ Transfer on Death Direction (TOD Form) have been reviewed. The records show that H. J. Druyvesteyn (the deceased) executed two TOD forms as follows:

- TOD Form executed Jan. 28, 2004, naming Terry Druyvestein as beneficiary

- TOD Form executed July 21, 2004, naming Lois Druyvesteyn as beneficiary

The above referenced account should have been changed to reflect your name on it as of July 21, 2004. As it was not, Summit is now in the process of correcting the Information at this time.

I apologize for any confusion or inconvenience this may have caused. Please contact Donna Young to discuss the disposition of this account.

If you have any other questions concerning this matter, please reply to the address below or email me at (email)

Respectfully,

Michael Sk. Hill
Exc. Vice Pres.
Chief Compliance Officer

Cc: Donna Young, CFPl
     Terry Druyvestein

What a shock this was to me. They did not even have the courtesy to address a letter to me, the person who was receiving the monthly account statements for the past six months and also the person who had put off cashing the bond to allow it to be cashed at par. I was the person for whom a new account was opened just for the purpose of processing this very bond and I now am notified of an error by receiving a copy of the letter sent to the new beneficiary. This was beyond belief. I can only imagine the shock Lois got when she received this letter. Her shock was probably one of glee rather than the disappointment I was now having.

So this letter was written 12 days before and now I receive a copy of it? It is obviously in error. How can I correct this? Is it already too late and has Lois cashed the bond in? How could they take my name off of this account and not even contact me except by copying me with a way over due letter? I needed some answers and I needed them fast. I called Donna Young to find out how this could be. Donna informed me that a mistake had been made and she knew her clients well and Humpy always wanted my family to have this bond. She would testify to this if needed. She said perhaps I should call Lois as she also knew this to be the case and perhaps we could work this out. If Donna was truly concerned, why had she not called me or notified me by mail? Things do not add up.

I called Lois's cell phone but could get no answer. So I called Lois's granddaughter in Ft. Smith who I had talked with and had met once on a drive Loretta and I took with Lois and Humpy. She said that their family had little to do with Lois anymore but she thought that Lois was at her daughter Linda's home in Oklahoma. She gave me the phone number for Linda.

I called Linda and she informed me that Lois was in the hospital with a leg injury. I explained to Linda that we had a problem with an error in the account held in my name and that I needed Lois's help to straighten it out. Linda said that she was aware of the situation in the letter from Summit but felt that it was "Summit who screwed up the records and it was therefore up to them to fix them." I said that I knew it was Summit's fault, but that I needed help from Lois to straighten the records out. I then gave Linda the phone number of Donna Young, and asked that Lois give her a call to confirm what needed to be done to correct the situation. Linda said that she would relay the message to Lois but would not give me a phone number so I could call Lois directly.

I was in a quandary as to what, if anything would happen with Lois calling Donna. In a couple of days, I called Donna to see if she had heard from Lois. She said that she had not heard anything. I tried calling Linda again but could never get her to answer nor call me back. I was working out of town and asked Loretta to call her during the day. Loretta did call and got an answer from Linda. They discussed the situation and Loretta passed on my concerns for the bond and my family. Linda told Loretta that they "did not want nor were they trying to get our bond money."

The next day I called Linda again and surprisingly she answered my call. It was not a bad conversation but Linda said that she was not going to receive any more of my calls and if I needed any more information, I should call her attorney. She then gave me her attorney's name and phone number, Mr. Roy Gean Jr. located in Ft. Smith, Arkansas. So now instead of ever talking to Lois, I had all of my dealings with Linda her daughter. I decided that I had better "lawyer up" as they say.

I decided to call one of my son's friends who I well respected, and who had become a lawyer and was working for a firm in Missoula, Montana near to our home. He had a few years of experience under his belt and worked for a reputable firm. Shane arranged for a conference call between me and Donna and himself. Shane asked specific questions of Donna as to what had gone wrong with the designation of me as TOD on Humpy's bond account. Donna seemed flustered, but eventually said that Humpy had taken the TOD designations home with him and brought them back but had not gotten Lois to notarize them properly! This seemed screwy to me as Donna is a notary. Well, she did not understand it entirely herself but the attorney for Summit Brokerage, a Mr. Hill who she worked with, said that the transfer of the bond to me as TOD was not done properly. I asked her if Humpy had changed his mind to give it to my family. Donna answered "not to my knowledge" and that she knew her clients well and was certain that it was Humpy's wishes that we receive the bond. She just could not understand what had gone wrong. Donna is an independent financial advisor and works through Summit to obtain her investments.

After Shane's discussions with Donna, he advised me to get an Arkansas Lawyer to handle the case for me as he was not licensed in Arkansas and was not familiar with their laws. He did check out the notary requirement as he felt certain that a notarized signature was not required for a TOD designation on a bond for which the spouse was not named as a co-owner. It turned out that Lois's notarized signature was not required. However, I needed to get an Arkansas lawyer. He looked though some statistics which the bar association publishes as to the type of case we might have and picked three of the top lawyers, statistically, in the State of Arkansas. He gave me their names and phone numbers.

I was in a rush. Mr. Gean, hired by Linda, had placed a call into Donna to get the papers worked out so Lois could cash in the bond. I had to get a lawyer on board to stop these proceedings. I called two of the names on Shane's list. Both were from Fayetteville, which is a short distance north of Ft. Smith. Both secretaries indicated that their boss was not in and asked if I wanted to leave a message, so I did and gave a brief description on my problem and asked them to return my call ASAP. I even called back the next morning as I had not gotten a response from either, and requested that they please call me back today. Another day was passing with no response so I called Jon Rose to ask if he knew any good attorneys. He said that he had just hired a good one a few months ago as he had a problem with Lois making off with a lot of their property from Humpy's house. He said he was a young man, but did a good job for them. His name was Troy, and he gave me his phone number. Having not made any headway with the reputable attorneys in Arkansas, I called Troy at the very end of the day. Troy shared my concern and said he would call Donna immediately and advise her that we were contesting the release of any funds from Humpy's bond fund on which I was named as the TOD and that he would be serving them with the necessary paperwork the next day. I felt relieved as I was finally getting something accomplished.

# CHAPTER FIVE
## The First Case

Troy got to work on my case right away. He asked how I wanted to pay for his fees. I had the option of paying "as we go" at an hourly rate plus expenses, or I could sign an agreement in which he would take a "contingency fee" of 1/3rd of whatever he collected for us. I asked him how much it would likely cost to pursue a court case against Lois and get a settlement. He said that legal fees for a case to be heard by a judge would likely run about $12,000, give or take a few thousand. I looked at this as a "no-brainer." With the accrued interest the bond would likely be worth about $210,000 so a third would cost our family $70,000. There was no doubt in my mind that we would win this case and even if I had to travel to Arkansas, it was likely that I could keep costs below $20,000. I told Troy that I was on board for the monthly billings and that I would send him a retainer for $2,000 to get started.

On November 27, 2007, I received a letter from my attorney Troy that a court order had been sent to Summit Brokerage and signed by Lois's attorney, Roy Gean Jr., directing them not to distribute any money from the account of Humpy's until our case was resolved. This court order would prevent them from making any illegal distributions, or so I thought.

It took until January 21, 2008 for Troy to study the case and give me his recommendations. Troy had received all of the documents from Summit Brokerage and studied them with these conclusions: In January of 2004 the account was placed in my name and then in July of that year, the account was removed from my name and placed in Lois's name. Yes, well, this I already knew. Troy said that the following is what concerned him about our case:

"We will have to argue that either she (Lois) unduly influenced him (Humpy) and basically forced him to change the accounts over into her name in July or we will have to argue that Humpy was incompetent in July when he signed them over. The thing that concerns me is that I think our best argument is incompetence because from talking to witnesses and the rest of his family, I think there is a decent argument that he was incompetent at this time. But I do not think that we can succeed in an incompetence argument because these two dates (designating you as TOD and then removing you as TOD) are so close together. It is not an effective transfer in July of 2004 if he was incompetent, but at the same time we would then have to argue that he became incompetent between January of 2004 and July of 2004. The reason we would have to argue that is because your transfer would also be invalid if he was incompetent in January when he put the account in your name as pay on death beneficiary."

In my letter hiring Troy and sending him a $2,000 retainer I had emphasized that Humpy and my family were still very close and based on all of my conversations with him that I knew that Humpy wanted me to get the bond and to spread the proceeds to our family. There never was any indication that he had changed his mind and that I was certain he hadn't intentionally done anything to change these plans. I also knew, having talked to the Rose family numerous times when Humpy was placed in the hospital, that they were certain Lois was a controlling, evil gold digger and was out to end Humpy's life as soon as possible so she could start living the life she envisioned when she married him. This was also supported by the views of his close friend Hub, in his letter to me where he wrote, "Lois never liked for us to be together when she was not there with us. I wanted to tell Humpy what she was doing but was afraid it would hurt his feelings as she was pretty slick at what she was doing."

As mentioned previously, Jon Rose had initially hired Troy as his attorney in their case against Lois for recovering property which she had illegally removed from their house. Humpy had willed his personal vehicles and house and all of his real estate property to his previous family. This was the Rose family which Humpy had formed with his previous wife, Bobbie. Lois had managed to cut all of Humpy's previous family and friends off from his presence but she could not change the Last Will and Testament, which had settled most estate matters ahead of time, and this did not include Lois. Humpy had taken care of her with life insurance, at least one bond, cash and two duplexes which were meant to be used for income for both of them and if it so happened that Humpy would pass away first, for Lois after he was gone. It was now apparent that Troy's involvement in the previous case with Jon, had exposed Troy to the true nature of Lois and it was influencing his views on the current litigation.

While I had a part of me wanting to expose Lois for who she was and what she had done, there was also a part of me that said "This may not be entirely true and even if it is, it will be a hard thing to prove". No doubt Lois was a "gold digger" but could we prove she was out to end his life? I also knew that Lois kept Humpy's old friends and family away and no doubt controlled every aspect of his life, and this continued to increase as my uncle became weaker and unable to defend himself. I guess I would have to listen to my attorney as he was the "authority" in the law. There would be several points of the law, I presumed, that we would pursue to obtain justice against Lois. I expressed my concerns to Troy regarding the undue influence and coercion and reiterated my concern that something must have been done to change the documents or that a simple mistake had been made. A simple but very important mistake!

On February 17, 2008, I became concerned when I had not heard from Troy. I emailed him and got a response. Troy had been taking treatments for a brain tumor and was nearing the end of treatments. He planned to be back in the office by February 28, full time. On one hand I was shocked but glad that he was doing well. On the other hand, I was wondering if it would affect his future performance on my case. What kind of treatments was he having? Would it affect his ability to think well? I decided that he needed support right now and we would proceed until there was some reason in the future to think otherwise.

Troy now let Summit Brokerage off the hook so to speak. I was amazed. They just may be the reason for the mistake but Troy said that we had no choice. The mistake, if one was made, had been made in July of 2004. The letter naming Lois as the TOD was sent to her in August of 2007. This was just past the three-year statute of limitations concerning this type of error. There was nothing which could be done now and besides, Troy needed Donna's testimony along with the Rose family that Lois was putting undue pressure on Humpy in the last year of his life. Here we go again with the coercion and the undue focus on that aspect of the case. I wondered how there could be a statute of limitations which started running on an error which was not even known at the time. It would appear that under the law, one is not liable for an error as long as you don't know about it. Do financial institutions just keep from "knowing" about something until the statute is exceeded? If they find out about an error, can they just bury it for a few more months until they can reveal it without fear because then, time would have expired on their liability? It was appearing to me that Summit Financial actually had discovered the error when preparing for the cashing out of the bond in April. Donna therefore missed the deadline to cash the bond in April and delayed for another five months or until the letter to Lois naming her as TOD was written at the end of August. There were lots of things that I did not like about this arrangement to basically give immunity to Summit Brokerage in exchange for Donna Young's testimony. I of course, had no proof of Summit Brokerage doing any of this intentionally.

Troy also said that we should hire a handwriting specialist. We needed the testimony of a specialist so we could show forgery by Lois. This coupled with testimony from Donna and the Rose family would basically clench our case. Well this was a possibility, that Lois signed the papers and not Humpy. I knew that Humpy did not wish to change them, so it could be a forgery. I told Troy to continue on and hire a handwriting specialist.

Troy would have to get the "original documents" from Summit Brokerage in order to have his handwriting specialist make a determination of authenticity. He thought this would cost about $600 and if the specialist thought the signature fraudulent, he would prepare a report for the court and of course come to testify. Besides attorney fees, costs were starting to add up.

The first person Troy wanted to depose would be Donna Young. He also wanted to get a deposition from Lois and perhaps he could do them on the same day so I would not have to come down to Ft. Smith twice. We would need a court reporter and at least with Lois, this cost would be shared equally. He figured the cost for the court reporter would be about $500. Troy thought that these two arguments, Donna Young's potential mistake and the forgery argument would either make or lose the case. I thought the deposition of Lois to be bigger. How could Lois deny that she was in Humpy's living room in 2006 (two years after the bond was supposedly changed making Lois the new TOD) when Humpy gave his instructions to me regarding the bond. How could she deny that she told me directly that I should "also thank her" for getting the bond for our family? How could she deny that she called and asked my sister Karen if we had cashed our bond in yet? This call to Karen took place several months after Humpy's death. Also, if she even thought the bond had been switched into her TOD name, why did she not mention it to Donna Young? Why did she not cash it in as she did with her other bond? These were all big things to me as it would require Lois, under oath, to lie. I guess to the legal system that must be common practice, but I could not imagine that people would prefer to lie rather than tell the "truth." I guess we will have to wait and see how Lois will handle this.

I gave Troy a list of dates when I had other commitments and it would be hard for me to come for the depositions. I would be open about 2/3rds of the time in the next six months so we should be able to schedule things. As usual things do not always work out as planned. Do you find that also? Anyway we could not get Lois pinned down to a date and Troy needed to depose Donna so he scheduled hers to be first. Because of this, I would not attend in person and he had his assistant, Amanda Cox, conduct the deposition. Why Troy was not able to conduct the deposition himself I do not know, but perhaps, looking back, it would have been better for him to have done so. I mean that from the standpoint that you need firsthand knowledge of things if you are going to properly weigh their merit and present them in court.

Donna Young was deposed on May 23, 2008 at 10:35 AM at her office in Van Buren, Arkansas. Donna testified that she was an independent certified financial planner. She was not a branch of Summit Brokerage. She had worked with my uncle Humpy for about three years before starting her own firm, which was in 2004. Before that she had worked for Morgan Stanley and had Humpy as a client there. When she started her own business, she took several of her old clients with her, and Humpy was one of them. At Morgan Stanley, Humpy had two accounts. One was a bond on which Sue Rose was the TOD. The other was a bond on which Terry Druyvestein was TOD. When these accounts were brought over to her new company in January of 2004, paper work was required to bring them over into her new system. Humpy instructed her to change the TOD of Sue Rose to his wife Lois. He instructed her to leave the TOD for Terry as it was. She was asked if Humpy ever asked her to change these later. She said that no, he never asked them to be changed. The deposition of Donna continued:

QSo what accounts were set up when they came into your new firm?A We set up Account No. 8136 for the bond on which Terry had previously been named TOD and we set up a new Account No. 8134 for the bond on which Sue Rose had been previously named as the TOD.

Q So there were two accounts, one for each bond with each having a different TOD?
A Correct, these were formed in January of 2004.

Q So, according to the forms a new TOD was named in July of 2004?
A Yes, according to the forms Lois was designated as TOD of account 8136.

Q Why do you think this was a mistake?
A If both bonds had the same TOD we would have moved both bonds into the same account. I would not have changed TOD on this account because to change the TOD would have meant two identical accounts, that doesn't make sense.

Q So you would have transferred the bonds from 8136 into 8134?
A Correct, so the other account would have been empty. I would have had everything in one account, if that was what Humpy had asked me to do.

Q So after this time, did you have any conversations with Humpy?
A Absolutely.

Q Okay. What were those transactions about and conversations?
A We didn't have any transactions, but he would come in frequently and he needed to see if his dividend checks had actually gone to his bank. He had a number of dividend checks coming from three different sources and they were being direct deposited in the bank. I would go through his statements and reconcile things and make sure that all of his income was going to where it was supposed to go.

Q And was Lois with him on those occasions?
A Yes, always.

Q So Lois was with Humpy when the accounts were brought to you on January 28, 2004 and did you watch Humpy sign the documents?
A Yes, I did.

Q And so he never came in to you after January, 2004 to tell you that he want to make a change to transfer everything to Lois?
A No, and the account was never re-registered to Lois, so it was always registered TOD Terry.

Since Donna had been deposed on May 23, 2008 and I had not heard from Troy, I emailed him with a list of questions on June 10. He mailed me back immediately.

Terry

Sorry about the delays. I have been booked.

1) Donna's depo went great. Everything she said was favorable to us. Humpy always meant the $ to go to you and she recalls that clearly and she never knew any different.

2) I have been told Lois is in the hospital and very ill and that I won't be able to depose her for another month.

3) I got the originals from Summit in yesterday's mail. I have contacted the handwriting expert about how I should get them to him. I was ordered by the judge to keep them in my possession so I will have to get leave to release them to him once I hear from him and get a cost estimate from him.

4) The Young depo gave me a sense of hope. I would go to court now on what we have (Donna + the Rose family eager to testify that Lois controlled Humpy and coerced him to do things in her favor) and feel that we have a legitimate chance. The handwriting expert would be icing on the cake. I have used him in other cases. But he is a very straight shooter; he will not tell us what we want to hear. It will be an FBI type opinion.

Great, as far as I was concerned. As I said in the beginning, I consider myself to be an honest person. I would not want to be associated with an unprofessional hand writing expert. I thought the deposition looked great as Donna said that there was a mistake, no other way about that. The problem seemed to be one of proving that the mistake had been made, clearly enough for the judge to be convinced that the bond should be returned to my family.

On July 15, 2008, I sent an email to Troy.

Troy:

1) What is the status of the analysis of the handwriting expert?

2) What is the status of the Lois depo? I understand that Lois recently called a neighbor in her old neighborhood. She was concerned that her daughter Linda seemed to be going through her money too fast and she was considering suing her! She said that she had knee surgery but seemed to be OK. Is she using these medical reasons for stalling on the deposition or is it just as much with her attorney advising her? Her friends say she is not that sick.

On July 22, 2008, Troy responded.

Terry:

1) I have not heard from the hand writing specialist.

2) I have sent a notice of deposition to Lois. Her attorney keeps saying she is sick but I do not believe it. He is as hard to deal with as she is. So, I don't know who it is, Lois or Roy Gean Jr. I have given them one month to produce her. I have actually set a specific date. The result of this is that if they do not want to have her that day they will have to file a motion with the judge to quash my subpoena and present medical evidence at a hearing.

On Sept. 1, 2008, I sent an email to Troy.

Troy:

1) You were getting a court order to get Lois deposed. (She was given a month) What has happened? Do we need a private investigator?

2) What is the status of the hand writing specialist?

3) Is there a problem with this case that I am not aware of? With payments or finances?

On Sept. 2, 2008, Troy responded.

Terry:

1) What do you think about setting the case for a hearing and giving notice to Lois for a telephone deposition? The problem is that I

got a curve ball when I learned the date the account was assigned to you. Recall, I originally wanted to argue that Humpy was incapacitated when he signed the changes in the documents and use his medical records to prove that. But that was before I found out the closeness of the date of the change in TOD and that of initially signing the account to you. I therefore believe that we are unlikely to be able to pinpoint his mental decline to between those two dates. I therefore think that the course of action we should take is to argue undue influence. We would use Donna Young, yourself and the Rose family to testify that Humpy always wanted you to have the bond. We would then argue with testimony from all sources, how Lois prevented contact with friends and family in order to coerce Humpy into signing things over to her.

2) I wanted the hand writing expert to give me his report before I deposed Lois. It appears that the reason he has not sent me a report is that he wishes to save the cost of one which is not favorable to us. I will talk to him on the phone but it appears that he cannot with any certainty prove there was a forgery.

3) No, there is not a financial problem. You have been a good client and paid your bills promptly.

4) I wish to emphasize that you need to understand the reasons why I do not think the incompetency claim is viable and also that you understand what we will need to prove for undue influence.

I was dismayed that we seemed to be in the same place we were months ago, trying to prove incompetency or undue influence. To a simple man, a mistake had been made, plain and simple. Correct the injustice simply by correcting the mistake. Obviously, it seemed me, we were pursuing the wrong line of offense, but then I am not the lawyer.

On Nov. 17, 2008, I emailed Troy.

Troy:

1) I see you have asked for a change in the hearing date for our case. Does this mean that a trial date is soon?

2) My sister, Karen, has written down the facts of Lois's call to her following Humpy's death. Should I get a copy to you?

3) What about my idea of agreeing to put the money from the bond into a money market account? At least we would gain some interest and it would be secure as we go through this long process in the courts. I am also concerned that if the Ford bond is not cashed that Ford could file for bankruptcy protection like GM has already done and that this would further complicate things.

On Nov. 17, 2008, Troy replied.
Terry:

1) I am pretty sure the trial got set for January 30th and paper confirmation is in the mail to you.

2) Send me what your sister has written and if she is going to be a critical witness, I will get a later (February or March) date set for trial.

3) No response.

On Nov. 18, 2008, I emailed Troy.
Troy:

1) I am attaching the letter from Karen Spring, my sister, addressing what was said to her regarding the phone call from Lois soon after Humpy's death. I think she is a very credible witness and her testimony is worthwhile.

2) I hope we can get a trial date set soon. We can work around it and be certain we are prepared for it properly. Perhaps we should be there a full day ahead of time to prepare for it? Anyway, you get the trial date set and I will get the time programmed.

3) With respect to Summit Brokerage and Donna Young, we need to ask the following questions, at trial if nothing else.

A) When did Summit actually receive the form changing the TOD? Donna's records did not match theirs. How could this be? Humpy never dealt with Summit directly, always through Donna. So Mr. Gean, Lois's attorney, claims that Humpy may have changed the

TOD on his own? I do not believe this. Did Lois try to change the records on her own? I could believe that.

      B) Lois met with Donna shortly after Humpy's death to cash her bond in. Was the bond which was going to our family discussed? I think that it probably was. What was the tone of this conversation? Lois knew perfectly well where the bond was to go so ask Donna what was said.

The following statement was attached to the email to Troy regarding the Karen Spring statement:

"When Uncle Humpy died, Lois made it clear to my family that there would be a private service for my uncle and we (the Druyvestein family) were not invited. So, when Lois called me at our shop in Custer, I was surprised to hear from her and especially since she had never called me before. After a few minutes, Lois said she needed to talk to my brother, Terry, and was calling for his phone number. I was quite certain she already had his phone number but I looked it up and gave it to her. She said that was the number she had but hadn't been able to reach him and she needed to talk to him because the Roses were contesting Uncle Humpy's will and the disposition of his assets. She was very upset about that and after awhile she said she didn't know why they were coming after her since Uncle Humpy had left Terry twice as much as he had left her.

Because I had no desire to be drawn into taking sides in her dispute with the Roses over Uncle Humpy's will, I told her I really didn't know anything about his will or who would inherit what. She seemed to be surprised that we hadn't discussed this inheritance but went on to say that it was worth a great deal of money and Uncle Humpy had made Terry the beneficiary. I don't recall if she ever specifically said what the inheritance was but she said Uncle Humpy had left it to Terry and she was sure he would share with the rest of us (my brothers and sisters); at least she hoped he would. After a bit more discussion about how she was doing, etc., she hung up saying she intended to call Terry."

To me this phone call clearly supported my contention that a mistake had been made. Lois knew exactly how Humpy had directed her and me as to who was to get this bond. This is what Humpy told us in his home in the spring of 2006, two years after the date when the TOD was supposedly changed. Lois clearly did not know about the error with respect to the TOD at the time she talked with Karen and it would be four or five months later, when Summit discovered the conflict in their files, and notified Lois that she evidently had been designated as the TOD. Lois and her daughter Linda then hired an attorney Roy Gean Jr. to go after the money. There no longer was any sense of what Humpy directed to be done, no sense as to how justice could be found. There was now only the realization that with a slick attorney they could make a case for the money. To some that is called legal, I would call that greed.

On Dec. 3, 2008, I emailed Troy.

Troy:

1) I understand that we will go to trial on Jan. 30. This will be a Friday. Is this a firm date that I can make plans around? I have checked airline connections and they are not good. I will drive down and come early so we can meet and plan things. (I checked maps and found the drive to be 1,797 miles and estimated 26 hours driving time, if roads were good.)

2) I trust you received the letter from my sister Karen. She may not be available to readily testify and perhaps it would be best to take her deposition or perhaps some kind of sworn statement?

3) When will we get together to plan for the trial? I would assume that it would be just prior to the trial date so everything can be fresh in your memory but also we need to know if there are people or statements needed now so we can have them available at the trial. Anyway, I am not too familiar with what to expect so perhaps you can outline what you will need to do to prepare for the case so I can help in any way that I can.

On Dec. 17, 2008, Troy responded.

Terry:

1) No response directly.

2) If Karen is going to be a witness, we will have to take a sworn statement by telephone with Roy Gean Jr. present. We cannot use the written statement. We can decide on the 31st if it is worth the money to do that.

3) Could you set aside an hour on December 31st? That is New Year's Eve of course. We could do it any time that day you want except we will close office at 4 PM. I will try to have Jon Rose available also. Perhaps we can do it in the morning as Jon runs the liquor store and the afternoon may be a big day for his sales. We can plan the overall trial at this time and then when you come down before the trial we can go over final details. I was looking at the Wednesday before the Friday trial as I have already scheduled to be in court on Thursday.

Well, I could see this guy is busy. To schedule a conference call on New Year's Eve was, should I say, "impressive." (It may also mean that he is over booked or too busy and does not have the time to cover his bases properly, I hope not.) So he wanted a time before 4:00 his time (Central) which would be 3:00 (Mountain). Good, the earlier the better.

I responded by email on Dec. 18, 2008.

Troy:

"Yes, I can be available on the 31st for a conference call. The morning would be best, say around 8 AM my time. That would be 9 AM Central. If you want to talk earlier I can do it at 8 AM your time.

Yes, I would like to have Karen testify. I guess we will decide that for certain on the 31st. She can be reached at her home at (xxx xxx xxxx) before the end of the year and perhaps a few days the first week of the next year. You can then use her cell (xxx xxx xxxx) after the first week of 2009.

Yes, I think Jon Rose knows a lot about the controlling nature of Lois and should testify. Also Bob or/and Sue Rose if you think it is needed. Humpy's best friend Hub is also a possibility but we can discuss that on the 31st. Donna Young is a must. I'm not certain who in her or the Florida office can answer the question as to when the change in beneficiary form was actually recorded into the files. Well, I guess we will discuss all of this on the 31st. Hope you are doing well and wish you and your family a blessed Christmas season."

Dec. 31, 2008, Conference Call

Troy was primarily focused on the need to show undue influence on Humpy and this mind set would indicate that Humpy did indeed change the records and remove me as the TOD for his account. The argument was basically that yes, he did change the TOD as the records show, but he did it under undue influence. Undoubtedly the Rose family was also behind the idea that Lois had taken control of Humpy's life near the end as she had completely taken charge of all of the decisions which Humpy was making. This was evident in what she had done both before and after Humpy's death. The only problem with all of this thinking was that the change to the TOD was made almost three years prior to his death.

Before Humpy died he was brought to the hospital, where Lois had refused treatment for him and had not allowed anyone other than herself to make any decisions as to his care. Humpy's best friends were not allowed to be with him, especially alone. Lois had built a wall between Humpy and all of his past friends and family. She may have even hastened his end by preventing him from getting the best of treatment. To many, Lois's motive was to get Humpy out of the way so she could finally get on with her life along with the money she needed for it.

I never could understand why Lois had Humpy buried in her family's cemetery plot with her spot reserved between her first husband and now Humpy. When Loretta and I visited, less than one year before Humpy passed away, both Lois and Humpy gave strict instructions that Humpy was to be buried lying next to Bobbie his previous spouse, and Lois was to be buried next to her past husband. Then Lois changed all of these plans by not allowing anyone to come to the funeral, as it was just for "close friends of her family." She had to know this would piss off all of Humpy's friends and past family, but then, I think that was her purpose. She wanted to leave a clear message that "SHE" was now the head of the family and "SHE" was calling the shots. It did not take long for her to exercise her authority. She immediately took not only all of the property she felt due to her, but also proceeded to take things that had been designated to others. Fortunately, most of these items were spelled out in a will or had been covered by previously changing titles of ownership. There were some things, smaller items such as my grandfather's chair and the family clock and Humpy's shotgun that would have no title.

There are many things collected in one's lifetime that have value only to specific people. That is why there are family heirlooms which are passed down only through selected family members. We expect these people to preserve these items, keep them for all to appreciate and eventually to pass them down along continuing family lines. These items were not appreciated by Lois. This was apparent in how she passed Humpy's shotgun down to her minister. I, on the other hand, really wanted it. It meant a lot to me and now hangs above my fireplace along with the shotguns or rifles of four other members of my family. Humpy's shotgun reminds me of the pheasant hunting days when I was young. My dad's shotgun is just above his. I have one grandson who will receive them when I pass on. It is already decided, just as it had been previously decided by Humpy. This had no meaning or value to Lois.

Troy and the Rose family were focused on the very bad behavior of a "gold digger" wife. I also felt the need to get back at her for the way she treated Humpy and for the way she snubbed the family after Humpy's passing. This however, must not be my primary motivation. Getting even is never the way to go with anything. It could also blind me from finding out the full story as to what had happened. The selfish motivation of Lois was definitely one part of the puzzle, but there had to be more.

Finally, Troy said we needed to be prepared to make a settlement offer as the judge will ask if we have tried to compromise, to settle the matter without further expenses for a trial, etc. Now that talk just sort of irks me about our system. When one is in the right, why should one have to settle for a lot less just because one has the threat of spending a lot more on legal fees just to get justice? Why doesnâ€™t the losing party have to pay all legal expenses on both sides? I think that it is done that way in at least some other countries. The reason we have so many attorneys in the United States is a result of this practice. It is argued that if one has the threat of having to pay legal fees for both sides, then a poor person will not want to bring suit even though he/she has a strong case. That is a somewhat legitimate argument but it does not hold water in many instances. Lawyers justify their exorbitant fees that are based on a contingency of 33 and even up to 50 percent to "cover the cost for cases in which they lose." It just shows me that many cases are brought into a "court," which should never have been there in the first place and this costs a lot of people a lot of money. Not just the complainant, but also the defendant, especially in a frivolous lawsuit.

A case in point: As I mentioned earlier, I was in the engineering and surveying business for over thirty years. Our company entered into a contract with a construction company to complete surveying for a highway construction project. The construction contractor had obtained a contract with the Montana highway department to build a new highway over Rogers Pass in northwestern Montana. During the course of this project, a worker for the construction contractor claimed that he had hurt his back while working as a laborer on the clearing of timber for the road reconstruction. The worker claimed that a "widowmaker" had been left by the surveyors on the project and that the contractor had not provided a safe environment for him to work in. A "widowmaker" is a term used in the timber logging business to describe a situation where a tree that has been cut hangs up in the branches of another tree. When the other is cut, presumable in this case by an unsuspecting worker, the unknown hung up tree becomes dislodged and falls upon the unsuspecting worker, often killing him. So in typical legal fashion, the lawyer for the victim names everyone in the case as defendants – the Highway Department, because they allowed an unsafe condition to develop; the construction contractor for not providing a safe place to work; and the surveying company for leaving a "widowmaker" when they were clearing the survey line. The suit claimed damages for five million dollars for pain and suffering, for loss of ability to work, and I don't remember what else.

My company, as the surveyor on the project, was served notice that we were being sued. We in turn contacted our insurance company to let them know they may need to defend us. I summoned all of our surveyors who had worked on the project to find out if we could have left a "widowmaker" in the field. Our guys were well versed in their work and I doubted that the claim was true. Person after person who worked on the project denied having even used a chainsaw on the part of the project where the accident supposedly happened. I say "supposedly" happened because firstly, the general contractor has a safety officer who all accidents have to be reported to; and secondly, a report would have been made out for the accident. None of this had been done. The worker did not know the full extent of his injury until the next morning when he had to go to his doctor. Anyway, our guys said they did not do it. The area where the accident happened had been previously surveyed by the State Highway Department crews and no additional clearing of survey lines was needed on our part. In addition to that, the rights-of-way agreement which the State had with the adjacent land owners, allowed the land owners to cut any timber from their property before the construction contractor proceeded with the final clearing.

Our company petitioned the Court to be released from being named in this suit. We were denied. So our company proceeded to gather work records, testimony from our workers, and in general to respond to a never ending request for information. We also hired a private investigator to find out some information on the man who had brought this lawsuit. We found out that he had come to Montana from Illinois where he had been awarded a rather large settlement with his last employer. You guessed it, for a back injury. We also found that the guy was taking his family fishing most days and hoisting coolers, tackle boxes, etc. into his boat. I thought to myself, this guy is simply a scam artist. Scam or not, I found that none of this information would be admissible in a court of law as it might prejudice the jury. Wow! A guy's track record is not admissible but my track record with respect to safety violations and response to correcting safety issues is perfectly permissible. Fortunately, we had a good safety record. Anyway, they were going to have a hard time showing that we had anything to do with injuring this person, if in fact he had been injured at all.

The case drags on for years. Produce more papers, answer more questions, take more depositions from employees. Finally, in a pretrial settlement conference which the judge had ordered, my company was asked what we would pay to end the case. My answer, "Nothing." The State Highway Department was represented as was the construction contractor. We did not negotiate together so I do not know what offers they made. My insurance company said that "nothing" was not acceptable. They ponied up with an offer of $5,000. The "injured party" – and I use that term loosely – took the offer. That figure, down from the original five million is quite a discount. All I know is that it cost me a lot of money in lost time and worry to clear my company from this frivolous lawsuit. Unfortunately, this is how our system works. We have to spend a lot of time and money just because we have no alternative. Judges rarely, and almost never, award a defendant legal fees for a frivolous lawsuit. It would cut down too many cases and too much of the overall revenue needed for our legal system to operate.

So a settlement offer was not something I wished to make with regard to the case with Lois, where I was certain that I was in the right and I had "truth" on my side. I also did not wish to diminish the value of something which was rightfully my family's, and by doing so disappointing my Uncle Humpy who had entrusted me to carry out his wishes.

Email to Troy, Jan. 4, 2009.

Troy:

1) I have been thinking about your request that we make a settlement offer to Lois. I do not like this concept and have a couple of questions.

A) I know that Lois cannot truthfully, under oath, testify as to her claim of ownership to the bond. After the July 2004 alleged change in TOD, Lois was present when Humpy met with Donna Young on a number of occasions to go over bank accounts and basically all of his financial holdings. Humpy never indicated that the bond was to go to anyone else, and in fact, Humpy went out of his way to emphasize that things needed to be in order with respect to me being the TOD. Donna Young will testify to this point. Also, Lois was present in early summer of 2006, when Humpy talked to my wife Loretta and me and told us all how he wanted these things distributed. At this time, Lois affirmed what Humpy had just told me by telling me that "You can also give me some thanks for getting the bond to your family." Lois also told me the same thing with respect to the bond after Humpy's death. In addition, Lois called my sister Karen and repeated that the bond was to go to all of my family. How can she deny all of these conversations? She can only lie directly or not testify on the grounds that she is too ill. I worry that her lawyer will keep her from testifying and we will never have an answer to these questions.

B) Is it possible to check into the validity of her alleged illness? Should we hire a private investigator to check this out? She has called on her old neighbors complaining that her daughter was spending too much of her money. Also she had the duplexes in Barling which, as Humpy's spouse, I suppose she now has solely in her name. How are they managed? I know her son Lee, who was the builder for Humpy when they built the duplexes, has since had a falling out with Lois and Linda. What could this be over?

C) Can Lois actually get through this case without ever showing up to testify? I think our case is seriously compromised if we cannot make her testify. Is this their strategy?

2) If we were, in fact, to make an offer to settle, would it be because you feel we do not have a very good case? Or, is it because there is too

69

much at risk to go to a trial? I hate to say it but if we have to do it, I would not offer to settle for anything more than giving Lois 25% of the principal bond amount which would be a lump sum settlement of $50,000. I personally think this too generous. With that settlement offer, I want you to tell her attorney that we make the offer only out of our wishes to settle this without any further damage to relationships, and that she knows as well as all of my family, and Donna Young as well, what Humpy's wishes were. I have discussed this offer with some of my family members and will discuss it with the others if we proceed. My mother should also be in agreement but I am not wanting to worry her about this entire affair and perhaps will never have to tell her the details. She is in nursing home care and does not see things as clearly as she once did. Too bad this is dragging on and on as she would have been happy to get the news two years ago.

On Jan. 6, 2009, Troy responded by email.

Terry:

1) Lois will not be allowed to benefit from failing to appear in court. If she does not show up at court, then it will damage her case severely. The only way I can see her illness impacting your case is for her to ask for a continuance. That will be inconvenient but it will not ruin our case. I have today written a letter to her attorney, telling him how far you are traveling and that I need to know immediately if she is going to claim her health will not allow her to appear in court. Otherwise, we will ask for her to pay any costs incurred.

2) As for the strength of our case, I strongly believe you should be willing to settle for less than you have offered in your email. (75%) Regardless of whether Lois appears at court or not we have the burden to offer proof of several facts. That is proof, not just a suspicion. Sometimes I think that non-attorneys have a hard time understanding how difficult it is to meet a burden of proof. Even if we all believe something is true, having clear proof of it is another thing. For instance, if we have witnesses to testify that Lois was controlling of Humpy and that Humpy had always wanted you to have the money, that is not

clear proof that she coerced him to change the form. It makes common sense to you and me, but it does not meet the legal definition of proof. Your sister's testimony will help along this line so I do want to do her telephone deposition. I will have that set up in a day or two.

3) Another option we have is to introduce evidence that Humpy was not in his right mind at the time of signing the change form. But the problem with that is that Humpy signed Lois's document only six months after your document. So, we would have to prove that his mental health declined in those six particular months, not sooner and not later.

4) Our only other case is based upon the idea this was a simple mistake with the account number. But again we can't just say it looks like a mistake was made with the numbers because everyone says you were supposed to get the bond. We don't have any actual paper proof of that or anyone who can say exactly who made the mistake.

5) I am going to hold the letter about settlement for another day. If you are unwilling to go 2/3rds then I will send the letter with a 1/4th offer like you mention. But as your attorney, I recommend that you offer at least 2/3rds to settle this matter. I believe there is a risk you will not get anything if we do not reach a settlement.

I guess that I am just stupid. My attorney tells me that I must settle this case by proposing an offer of at least 2/3rds then he states that he believes "There is a risk that you will not get anything." Not much to be very confident about. The options are not good. The one option I think is viable, is simply that a mistake was made, but according to my attorney, "We can't just say it looks like a mistake was made with the numbers on the account," but we must have actual proof of that or someone who can say exactly who made the mistake. What is actual proof of a mistake? If there was actual proof, there would not be a mistake. You must rely, at least to some degree, on the testimony of those in charge as to what probably happened. There was testimony by Donna Young that they often had clients sign papers which had not yet been filled in with account numbers and even sent papers home which did not have the account numbers on them. They finished filling them out when they got them back, signed by the clients. Why is it so hard to prove a mistake when you have people on both sides of the case saying the same thing? You just need Lois's testimony. We need to get it. She knows what the truth is. Linda her daughter also admitted as much when she said, "We don't want to take "your" money." Lois called my sister and said to cash your bond in soon so the Rose family doesn't get it. The Rose family will also testify as to the fact that Humpy wanted the bond to go to my family. There is no argument at this point. Everyone agrees that the bond should go to my family. Why is this not sufficient? Because the brokerage company, after delaying any action in making a decision because of discrepancies with their account numbers, decides that they need to pass the three-year statute of limitations before bringing this to light. They do this by missing the anniversary date for cashing in the bond and then wait an additional five months to expose their mistake, thus avoiding any potential lawsuit against them. They are the ones who should really be defending their actions, but they are left off the hook.

I needed to collect my thoughts and try one last time to get my points across to my attorney. I believe that Troy is so focused on exposing Lois for what she is that he is missing the main point of our argument. I do not believe Lois was aware of the fact that there was a problem with the TOD designation forms and that she did not commit an act of forgery nor was she able to coerce Humpy by managing a change from my name to hers on the TOD form. By all accounts, she did not know of the apparent mistake until she was notified by Summit Brokerage in their letter to her on August 28th, 2007.

So what really did happen? I had to get my head into this and try to figure out a logical explanation. I needed some proof as Troy would say. I started with how all of this came about.

After Donna Young started her own business, she testified that she had worked at Morgan Stanley and brought some of her own clients over to her new company. Humpy was one of these clients and on January

28th, 2004, Humpy and Lois went into Donna's office and opened two new accounts. One was No. 8136 and one was No. 8134.

It was clear from Donna Young that the two accounts were serviced by mail on a monthly basis from 2004 through Humpy's death in 2007 as follows:

A. Account No. 8136 addressed as follows:

> H. J. Druyvesteyn
> TOD Terry Druyvestein
> 607 6th Street
> Barling, Arkansas 72923

B. Account No. 8134 addressed as follows:

> H. J. Druyvesteyn
> TOD Lois Druyvesteyn
> 607 6th Street
> Barling, Arkansas 72923

Now, because these were both Humpy's accounts, and on a monthly basis he and Lois would receive interest checks, would it not be obvious that he or Lois would have noticed that the TOD was in error? If they had indeed wanted to change the TOD they would have gone in and asked Donna to change the TOD from Terry to Lois on account 8136. But it was left like this for almost three years after the date that Summit Brokerage now says the TOD had actually been changed? Especially, would not Lois have noticed this very obvious error in the TOD of account No. 8136? Is this not "proof" of how it was supposed to be? I guess I do not understand what Troy needs for "actual proof."

Also from the testimony of Donna Young, the point was made that all accounts brought into her new company from Morgan Stanley, had to be brought in exactly in the same format as they existed at Morgan Stanley. Any changes that were made in TOD or anything else, even mailing address etc., could only be made "after" the new account had been created by bringing the Morgan Stanley account in exactly how it existed at Morgan Stanley. Donna also testified that at Morgan Stanley one account was already designated as TOD Terry Druyvestein and the other account was designated TOD Sue Rose. Donna testified that Humpy wanted the new account, 8136, to remain TOD Terry. She also testified that Humpy wanted to change the other account, 8134, which came over as TOD Sue Rose, to TOD Lois. If this were the case, it is also true that a change in TOD would have to be made to drop Sue Rose and make one account TOD Lois. In the documents bringing over the two accounts (dated January 28, 2004) both are checked as an original application of beneficiary. Account 8136 is marked for Terry and account 8134 is marked for Lois. There was no change in beneficiary marked in the account No. 8134 which would have allowed the account to be switched from Sue to Lois. This was probably an oversight and was corrected later, in the July 21, 2004 paperwork, and this in all probability, was mistakenly assigned to account No. 8136. So the result is that there are now two accounts which, according to Summit Brokerage, are TOD Lois, but there is only one TOD designation form. Donna also strongly stated that she would never have made two accounts if the TOD for 8136 had been changed to Lois. Rather she would have rolled both bonds into the same account. She stated that this would have been their standard practice, continuing with two accounts with the same TOD would "not make any sense" – her exact words. I believe that a few months after Donna Young created her new business, Humpy and Lois began receiving their monthly statements as:

H. J. Druyvesteyn
TOD Sue Rose

So a change in TOD form was requested to make it as Humpy and Lois wanted:

H. J. Druyvesteyn
TOD Lois Druyvesteyn

This is a scenario which made sense and Donna should be questioned as to if this is what probably happened. If we can ask Lois, this question should also be put to her.

I shared all of these opinions with Troy in an effort to get him focused on the task of providing "proof" of an error. It seemed that if proof was needed that we should go about finding the truth and that would start by questioning the people who probably knew what actually happened. Perhaps some of them needed to be prodded a little more to tell the truth. Isn't that what the justice system is all about? In any event I told Troy that I did not wish to proceed with the case on the basis of "undue influence" or coercion.

In an email of Jan. 20, 2009 to Troy:

Troy:

"As it now stands, we are planning to leave here on Monday, the 26th and travel by vehicle to Ft. Smith. We would arrive there on Thursday the 29th in the event that you can meet with us the day before the trial. Perhaps a few directions would help us get into the right neighborhood. I do not remember much of the area your office is in.

Perhaps I am a little out of touch with reality or perhaps I am just blinded by what I know to be the case, but I look at our case and it seems to me that we do have quite a bit of proof on our side.

Anyway, I hope we can talk Thursday about our case. Let me know your schedule."

I now would have three days to travel and think about our case. Hopefully I will not be distracted from my driving. I certainly have been taken out of my "sleep" mode. I guess that's par for the course.

# CHAPTER SIX
## The Trial

The 1800 mile trip from Rollins, Montana to Ft. Smith, Arkansas is not the trip to take near the end of January. Things started OK in Montana but after the initial 600 plus miles to Douglas, Wyoming it turned into a nightmare. Trying to get ahead of the game we bit off more than we wanted when we traveled 750 miles to Douglas on the first day. There was a blizzard roaring through Douglas when we arrived. We stopped at a Super 8 and got a room. I have an AARP card so we got a ten percent discount. The wind was blowing hard and the room was barely staying ahead of the game, temperature wise. In the morning we got up to snow drifts and in general a traffic mess with cars stranded along the streets and snow plows trying to clear the snow. We got an egg Mcmuffin from the Golden Arches with black coffee and headed out. The interstate was fairly clear and after a couple hundred miles we got ahead of the worst of the snow. The problem was it also got wetter and the snow stuck to the roads. We stopped for the night in southeast Nebraska where my youngest sister Virginia lived. Ginny, as our family calls her, was named after Humpy's first wife whose name was Virginia. We enjoyed the evening with her, stayed only for the night and headed out early Wednesday for Ft. Smith. Unfortunately, the roads got worse rather than better. We did not make it to Ft. Smith. After a grueling day we made it as far as Tulsa, Oklahoma. We were really glad that we had a four-wheel drive vehicle. We only had another 120 miles to Ft. Smith but in the morning when we left Tulsa there was hardly a vehicle on the road. The roads were not snow packed; I would liken it more to ice packed. It had warmed to the point that things were very slick. We pressed on through most of the morning and got to Ft. Smith around 11:00 AM. I had called and arranged to meet Troy right after lunch.

Troy was ecstatic when we arrived. Not exactly for meeting us, but rather he had been searching for a good answer to proceeding with our case and thought he had found the solution. He had abandoned the "undue influence" scenario and was fully committed to the idea that a mistake had been made and that there was, in fact, a way to approach this without the high burden of proof he had been thinking that we needed to prevail. We would have to approach the case under the LAW OF MISTAKE AND CONSTRUCTIVE TRUST. Under this concept about a mistake, one cannot become "unduly enriched by a mistake." Troy's research on the subject defined a mistake and a constructive trust as follows:

The law of mistake was virtually created by equity. Assume a bank credits a customer's account with $1,000 by mistake. The bank's action was not intentional, but a result of its own negligence or fault. The bank's claim against the customer is unjust enrichment. The court should impose a constructive trust on the $1,000 for the benefit of either the bank or the intended recipient, even if it is commingled with other funds of the customer.

So, what is the burden of proof to create a constructive trust?

Arkansas appellate courts have repeatedly written that a constructive trust requires clear and convincing evidence. This does not mean, however, that written proof is required or that all evidence must be without contradiction. In many of the cases Troy found, that written proof was not provided, but rather simply that the court was focused on the "unjust enrichment", which was a result of an apparent error.

This certainly fit our case I thought. The problem was that we would go to court tomorrow morning and there was very little time to get our case in order. Troy was absorbed in getting the facts together, as he now saw them through the eyes of a case for creating a "constructive trust." I really was not of much help in how he was going to get his points of law across to the judge. We talked some about who to call and in what order and what I would be asked to testify to. Also Loretta would testify and Jon Rose. The big testimony about a mistake would be coming from Donna Young. Lois would not be testifying nor would she be attending the trial. Her daughter Linda would be testifying in her stead. I wondered how Linda's testimony could be either reliable or truthful. Linda knew virtually nothing of the case and if asked questions would she even know what recollection Lois had of the subject? How could Linda's testimony be allowed and credited as accurate when she simply knows nothing first hand about the case? I did not like the short time period available to prepare for tomorrow, but soon enough, tomorrow would come.

On **Jan. 30, 2009 the Fort Smith District in the Circuit Court of Sebastian County, Arkansas** was brought to order by the Honorable James O. Cox. In the case of Terry Druyvestein V. Summit Brokerage Services, Inc. and Lois Druyvesteyn.

I wondered why the case still made mention of Summit Brokerage as a defendant as we had allowed them to withdraw as a liable party, but they were still a party which would testify at the case, so who am I to be picky? The testimony in the court case went pretty much as expected from the key witnesses. I will give you a summary of that testimony, based primarily on my notes and also the record of testimony from Judge Cox's decision in the case.

Terry Druyvestein:

I testified to the wishes of Uncle Humpy to have me become the TOD of a Ford Motor Company Bond when he passed away. Humpy called me on the phone sometime in 2003 to tell me this and that he was having his financial advisor contact me to get personal details on doing this. Donna Young contacted me about this within a week or two and the wish was executed by making me the TOD. We did not talk specifically about this for some time although I asked Humpy if he wanted me to tell my siblings at the 2004 family reunion but he indicated that may not be a good time to do this. I testified that we did discuss the bond in May of 2006 when we visited Humpy and Lois in Arkansas. I testified that Lois and my wife Loretta were present when Humpy discussed what he wanted done. We discussed the family heirlooms, his shotgun and the bond. He told me he wanted me to have the bond and I told him that I would plan to share it with my siblings. He told me "I know you will do what is right." I testified to the fact that when Humpy excused himself from the room that Lois reiterated that I could thank her for the bond also and I did so.

I testified to the fact that in our 2006 visit, Humpy and Lois drove Loretta and myself around the Ft. Smith area to where he and Lois were to be buried. We also went around to Camp Chaffee and many places of interest to their past. I testified as to how Lois went against these wishes, how none of the family was allowed at the funeral.

I testified as to how I was put on the account for the bond with Delta, how we tried but missed dates for the cashing in on the bond and then finally how I received the letter from Summit which was actually sent to Lois removing me as TOD for the bond. I testified to most of what you have read before and will not detail it.

Toward the end of my testimony, Troy threw me a curve ball. He said "Your Honor, Mr. Druyvestein has a theory on how he thinks this all came about!" "Objection!" says Mr. Gean, "This man is not an authority in these matters and has not been designated as an expert witness." Judge Cox says, "I'll allow it. Go on Mr. Druyvestein."

Wow! I was not prepared to put my theory into words. We had talked about this ahead of time but not in a format I could use to express it to the judge, and I had not rehearsed how I would put this all into words. I thought lawyers "never asked a question which they did not already know the answer to." Well perhaps Troy knew the answer but I was scrambling to put it all together. I started by going through the creation of the two accounts and how they first had to be brought in exactly as they were in Morgan Stanley, how that was not done correctly in the records, how probably the records had to be corrected. The judge said, "Mr. Druyvestein, you need to speak to me, not your attorney!" I was in the witness chair, nervous, and was addressing my story by looking at and speaking directly to Troy, who had asked the question. The judge, rightly so, was admonishing me for not looking at him when addressing the question. I was not making any points with this. Anyway, I got it back together and faced the judge and did my best to relate that there was no change in TOD from Sue Rose to Lois for the bond she had already cashed. That the TOD on my account (8136) was incorrectly changed and what Donna Young was attempting to do, was to correct the error on (8134) or Lois's account. There was only one TOD to Lois so she should only get one bond. Not both. I am afraid I should have arranged my testimony a little more clearly as it was a complicated testimony and had to be spoken clearly for someone else to understand. Obviously it went over the Judge because he completely ignored this testimony in his summary. Perhaps you are shaking your head as to what I just said also? I will clear this up later.

Loretta Druyvestein:

Loretta testified that she and Lois were present when Humpy talked to me about his wishes. She stated that Humpy wanted Terry to receive his Grandfather's chair, the family clock and the Ford Motor Company Bond. She also said that she was aware of the TOD designation when it happened. She called Linda about the mistake and discussed it with her. Linda agreed to look into this and they were not "trying to take our money."

Donna Young:

The testimony from Donna Young was even stronger than in her deposition that a mistake had been made. She even gave an educated guess as to why there was a conflict in the records which went along with the theory that the error was created by poor record keeping by Humpy's financial advisor, Donna herself. When asked how the document changing the TOD from Terry to Lois came about Donna answered:

"I have no explanation other than if my back office (Summit Brokerage) had called and said we need this for housekeeping reasons, such as: would you get them (Humpy and Lois) to submit some new forms on the beneficiary? Then I would have, at their next visit, asked them to sign the forms and then send them in. If the account still read TOD Sue Rose, then, you know, we would have had to change it. It would have been a housekeeping change, so we needed to get the records correct."

Continuing, Troy asked Donna: Is this your handwriting on exhibit #1, where someone wrote in the account number – 8136?

Answer, Donna: It looks like my hand writing.

The Court: Judge Cox weighing in: So which one are you talking about?

Answer: Exhibit #1, for account number 8136.

The Court again: So that's your hand writing?

Donna: It very well could be.

The Court: Okay.

Troy: Did you write that when you filled out that document? Did you do it with the intention to take Terry Druyvestein off of the account?

Donna: Absolutely not.

Troy: If you wrote this number on here (pointing at the exhibit) for the account number, did you do so by mistake?

Donna: Yes!

Donna testified further by stating she advised the legal department at Summit that her client (Humpy) never intended to take Terry's name off the account. Their attorneys, however, said that since they had a document signed by Humpy, they went by the document because that is what they are compelled to do. She stated that Summit lawyers told her that this is the way it would be "unless the judge decides otherwise."

(My notes: Donna was in court to do what she had to do in an effort to make things right. She was testifying in order to change the record by testifying to the "truth." The question now seemed to be, would the judge listen for the "truth."

Well, I thought, that all in all, this should be convincing enough testimony that a mistake was made. There was also much more testimony along the same lines which I have covered previously. I thought things were looking up.)

Jon Rose:

Jon testified that Humpy wanted the bond to go to my family. He testified that Humpy had taken care of his family and Lois and wanted my family to have the bond.

Linda Van Divner:

Linda testified to very little. She mainly said that her mother had physical problems and was unable to testify.

(My notes: Now this just does not seem right. We are having this trial because Lois has laid claim to monies from a bond which my Uncle Humpy had designated to go to my family. Lois was never made to testify, not by deposition and not by coming to this trial. I guess Lois's attorney got a letter from a doctor who said that she was not competent to stand trial. I never have seen a copy of this letter. I do know that several of Lois's neighborhood friends were contacted by Lois as she wanted to know what had been going on in her neighborhood, so at least initially Lois was OK to talk to. This litigation has now been going on for 15 months, so why has Lois not been at least deposed? Linda has said that her mother has been in an assisted living home. An assisted living home requires one to be at least competent enough to do lots of things on one's own. So Lois is not competent enough to do a deposition? I say that is not truthful. Troy has said that if Lois does not testify, it will hurt their case, not help it. I do not agree with this assessment as Lois is the only other person who knows the truth in this case, but I guess, if she got on the stand and lied, could she pull it off? I think there are too many people with the true knowledge of the situation that she would struggle to discount my testimony, Loretta's, Karen's, Jon's and Donna's.)

Mr. Hill, Summit Brokerage (from Judge Cox review of the testimony):

The deposition of Michael Hill was offered into evidence. His records reflect that with regard to the account in question (8136), the initial beneficiary as of January 20, 2004 was Terry Druyvestein. That was changed by H. J. Druyvesteyn on July 21, 2004, to Lois Druyvesteyn. Mr. Hill testified that the Change of Beneficiary Form done in July appeared to abide with their procedures. The earlier form from January did not. The problem with the January form was that the wife's signature was not notarized. Although her signature was not notarized the document was signed off on by the firm's chief compliance officer.

(My notes: Early on it was determined that a wife's notarized consent signature is not required on a document made out to and solely owned by the husband, so why does Mr. Hill keep using this as an excuse? I have to wonder if that omission was part of the reason why Summit stalled to surpass the statute of limitations before bringing this to anyone's attention. But there were plenty of other errors to go around, both with Donna Young's Delta Company, which she admitted to, and to her home office, Summit Brokerage.)

(Continuing with Judge Cox's summary of the testimony)

Mr. Hill testified that when he discussed the account with Donna Young, she told him that she thought Terry was the beneficiary the whole time, but he explained to her that he did not think Terry was, based on the forms received. Although she felt like it had been a mistake, he pointed her attention to the fact that the account holder put a check mark or an X in the change in registration form which made very clear the decedent's intent to change beneficiaries.

(My notes: Yes, Humpy put an X in the change in registration form because he thought he was changing account 8134, which was still in Jon and Sue's names as TOD. Does Mr. Hill only talk and never listen? I see this as a big problem with a deposition taken a long time ago, when my attorney was not even focused on there being a mistake and the constructive trust, and now we are not able to cross examine the witness as he was not required to appear at trial.

At the conclusion of the trial the court ordered that each party would be granted ten days to file Post Trial Briefs. The Plaintiff would have until February 9th to file their brief. The Defendant would then have until February 19th to file a Response Brief. The Plaintiff would then have until February 24th to file a Reply Brief.

I was nervous about the trial but felt pretty confident that we would get a positive ruling. I was still concerned that, for my part, I did not explain the details of the events creating and leading from the mistake that was made. I was afraid that at least part of any misunderstanding was my fault for not explaining things clearly enough. I prepared a timeline which would help in this matter and sent it to Troy hoping he could clear this up in one of his briefs.

Acct. No.
8134

Account @ Morgan Stanley
H. J. Druyvesteyn
TOD Sue Rose

**Jan. 28, 2004** Humpy asks Donna Young
to transfer this account over to her new
business, **changing** the TOD from Sue Rose
to wife Lois. Donna creates acct. No. 8134
with paper work **wrongly** showing Lois
Druyvestein to be the Original Applicant
for registration as beneficiary.

Statement for Acct. 8134 are addressed:
H. J. Druyvesteyn
TOD Sue Rose

**July 21, 2004**
No change in the beneficiary form is issued;
however, the account TOD is changed making
Lois the beneficiary.

Statements for Acct. 8134 are addressed:
H. J. Druyvesteyn
TOD Lois Druyvesteyn

**H. J. Druyvesteyn Passes**
Acct. statements are mailed to Lois and a new
Acct. is made for her funds. Lois decides to
cash her bond in. Acct. is terminated.
Lois does not inquire about Terry's bond.

**August 28, 2007**. Summit financial sends the
letter to Lois informing her that they had made
mistake and that she was the actual beneficiary
of acct. 8136 and that they would proceed
to transfer the acct. 8136 to her.

Acct. No.
8136

Account @ Morgan Stanley
H. J. Druyvesteyn
TOD Terry Druyvestein

**Jan. 28, 2004** Humpy asked Donna Young
to transfer this account over to her new
business, **keeping** Terry as the TOD for the
the account. Donna creates acct. No. 8136
showing **correctly** that Terry is the Original
Applicant for registration as beneficiary.

Statements for Acct. 8136 are addressed:
H. J. Druyvesteyn
TOD Terry Druyvestein

**July 21, 2004**
A beneficiary change form is wrongfully
filled out naming Lois as the TOD of this
acct.: however no change is made.

Statements for Acct. 8136 are unchanged:
H. J. Druyvesteyn
TOD Terry Druyvestein

**away on February 24, 2007**
Acct. statements are mailed to Terry and a
new acct. is set up. Terry does not cash in
bond as it trades below par and awaits the
new anniversary date to cash bond at par.

**July 21, 2007** The three year statute of
limitations is reached concerning the mistake made on the TOD form July 21, 2004.

Terry has lawsuit filed to stop injustice.

## TIMELINE FOR BOND ACCOUNTS 8134 & 8136

My theory is that after the 2004 Reunion, which was in early July, Lois got after Humpy to bequeath to her one of the bonds he was holding, on which they were now receiving interest. (A little over $2,000 per month) She would be in need of a little more cash in addition to the personal accounts and the property she now had coming to her in the event of Humpy's death. They go down to Donna and request she change the TOD on the bond which was in Sue Rose's name. They have Humpy sign the form for a new TOD and mark it as a change. The wrong account number is later placed on the form. There is only one change in beneficiary form and it is placed in the Sue Rose – Lois Druyvesteyn file. So the accounts are received each month and addressed as follows:

ACCOUNT NO. 8134
Name: H. J. Druyvesteyn:
Beneficiary: TOD Lois Druyvesteyn

ACCOUNT NO. 8136
Name: H. J. Druyvesteyn:
Beneficiary: TOD Terry Druyvestein

The account statements come to Humpy on a monthly basis and are labeled as shown. Lois is certain to check these and she is OK with them. This is the way everyone thought they should be and they are sent out this way for almost another three years. No one took issue with this. In April of 2007 it was discovered that there was a wrong file of designation of beneficiary in 8134. Lois had already been paid out. Sue Rose would be the rightful owner based on Mr. Hill's testimony. What to do? Wait till after the three-year statute of limitations runs out and put the TOD form into account No. 8136 and thereby change the beneficiary to Lois.

On February 9, 2009, Troy files his Post Trial brief and I am happy that we are now on the same page.

IN THE CIRCUIT COURT OF SEBASTIAN COUNTY, ARKANSAS
FORT SMITH DISTRICT
PROBATE DIVISION

| | |
|---|---|
| TERRY DRUYVESTEIN | PLAINTIFF |

VS.                    CASE NO. CV-2007-1383

| | |
|---|---|
| SUMMIT BROKERAGE SERVICES, INC. and LOIS DRUYVESTEIN | DEFENDANTS |

**POST TRIAL BRIEF**

I.    **Discussion of Facts**

I will not spend much.time on the facts of this·case because the case is fresh in the Comt's mind and the.Court took go.odnotes. H.J. Druyvestein had two bond accounts managed by Donna Young. Account# 2895-8134 and Account# 2895-8136. He told· Donna Young, Terry Druyvestein, Loretta Druyvestein, John Rose, and Lois Druyvestein, that he intended for Terry to have one bond and for Lois to have the other bond.

In January 2004 Donna Young left Morgan Stanley·anct went to Delta Financial where she worked as a broker for Summitt Financial. On January 28, 2004, Humpy signed documents to designate Lois as the transfer-on-death beneficiary for 8134 and Terry as the beneficiary for 8136.

On July 21, 2004, Humpyhad another meeting with Donna Young. He signed a "Change of Beneficiary". form in that.Jneeting that placed Lois on the 8136 account as TOD beneficiary. Donna Young was the only person to testify about this meeting. She testified that she was "certain" that Humpy did not want to take Terry off of any account in that meeting. She also testified 1hat she was "certain" that she made a mistake in writing down 1he 8136 account numbu on the change of beneficiary form. She testified that the reason a new form was filled out is "most likely" because Sue Rose had been the beneficiary on the Morgan Stanley assets which were put into the 8134 account Since assets have to be transferred from one broker to another in the exact same form, the 8134 account needed a Change of Beneficiary from Sue Rose to Lois. The key point is that Donna Young is adamant that this was a mistake and Humpy intended for Terry to inherit the 8136 account.

This mistake is corroborated by the following undisputed testimony:

a) Humpy told John Rose before and after July 2004 that Terry would receive a bond.

b) In 2006, Lois told Terry and·Loretta that they could "thank her" for 1he bond they would receive.

c) Humpy confirmed his wishes to Donna Young in numerous meetings after 2004.

d) Monthly statements were mailed to Humpy from 2004-2007 which said "TOD Terry Druyvestein." Neither Humpy nor Lois ever questioned this. Even after Humpy rued Lois did not attempt to collect on Terry's ac:<:ount until Summitt discovered the mistake document.

e) Wben Lois cashed in her bond, she did not ask to cash in the bond with Terry as TOD.

f) Terry and Humpy bad a strong relationship. Terry, as a blood relative is the natural bounty of Humpy's affection.

Troy's Post Trial Brief includes a summary of applicable law and if you wish to review the full document scan this QR CODE.

I received and email from Troy April 1, 2009. (April fool's day but this was no joke)

Terry:

"I got the judge's decision last night when I opened my mail at the house. He decided against us and I believe it is based on a misunderstanding of the law. He says that we must prove there was a mistake of one party accompanied by fraud on the other party. In short, he does not seem to question that Donna Young made an error but says that since there was apparently no fraud involved (in fact there may be as Lois thought the account was yours also) that he cannot create a constructive trust.

You have read my brief on the law. I believe it is very thorough on the law of mistake. I disagree with him and I think you can understand why from reading my brief. Read this judge's opinion that I am mailing to you today and decide if you wish to appeal the case. The negative side of appeals is that only about 20% have any success. But I do believe that an error was made here.

We have a deadline of April 26th to file the appeal by. The decision would take around 8 months to a year from that time. Please let me know how you would like me to proceed. I am sending the decision priority mail so you should get it soon."

-Troy

Well, in a way, this was a good response from Troy. He was getting 100% behind the fact (I said it was a fact but the Law did not go that far) that a "MISTAKE" was made. The discouraging part was that this would take another year and statistically at least, only about a 20% chance of success. I was wondering if my bank account would hold up. I received Judge Cox's decision and have given you the summary in his own words.

## James O. Cox
CIRCUIT JUDGE • DIVISION VI
TWELFTH JUDICIAL DISTRICT

SEBASTIAN COUNTY COURTHOUSE
901 S. B STREET, STE. 203
FORT SMITH, ARKANSAS 72901

TELEPHONE: 479-782-3035
FACSMILE: 479-784-1537

KIM DODSON
TRIAL COURT ASSISTANT
MAVIS McELROY
COURT REPORTER

March 26, 2009

Troy Gaston, Esq.
1405 West Center, 3rd Floor
Greenwood, Ark. 72936

Roy Gean, Jr., Esq.
511 Garrison Avenue
Fort Smith, Ark. 72901

RE:    Terry Druyvestein v. Summit Brokerage Services, Inc.
       And Lois Druyvesteyn
       Fort Smith District, Sebastian County Circuit Court
       Civil Division
       Case No. CV 07-1383 (VI)

Dear counselors:

   I appreciate the excellent presentation of the facts in this difficult case as well as your trial briefs. My analysis follows:
(I skip to the conclusions)

CONCLUSION:

   It is impossible for the court to peer into the minds of the parties involved in this case. It would be of great help if we knew what H. J. Druyvesteyn was thinking in 2004 when he signed his name to the legal document. It would likewise be nice to know what Lois Druyvesteyn thought, but we did not have the benefit of her testimony.

   Since we cannot look into their minds, we must look at their actions. The testimony that we have consisted of Plaintiff's in which he unequivocally stated that he thought all along that he was going to be the beneficiary of one of Mr. Druyvesteyn's accounts.

90

We have the testimony of Donna Young in which she appears to confess to making an egregious mistake that has affected the rights and interests of the parties in this case. Ms. Young's testimony is founded upon supposition, guesses and assumptions. She is the only person who offered any testimony with regard to the transaction and she is without any recollection of the events of the particular day Ms. Young's testimony was confusing at best and dissembling at worst.

Based on the testimony presented I cannot find by clear, cogent and convincing evidence a mutual mistake or a mistake on one party accompanied by the fraud on the part of anyone. If a unilateral mistake was made by Mr. Druyvesteyn it was not the product of any fraud but neglect. The fact is that the change was made and after the change was made Mr. Druyvesteyn discussed his account with Ms. Young, at least four times a year, according to her testimony. No further changes were made to the account. I find that the facts are much like the facts of the Trimble case cited above.

A file marked copy of my order is enclosed for your file.

Best personal regards.

Cordially,

James O. Cox

cc:   Sebastian County Circuit Clerk

(If you wish to review the full decision please do so by scanning the QR code below)

IN THE CIRCUIT COURT OF SEBASTIAN COUNTY, ARKANSAS
FORT SMITH DISTRICT
CIVIL DIVISION VI

TERRY DRUYVESTEIN                            PLAINTIFF

vs.            CASE NO. CV 2007-1383 (VI)

SUMMIT BROKERAGE                    DEFENDANT
SERVICES, INC. and
LOIS DRUYVESTEIN

## ORDER

Now on this 26th day of March, 2009 this cause comes on for decision, testimony having been taken previously. The Court, having had heard the testimony of the parties, having reviewed all of the exhibits offered into evidence and having the benefit of post-trial briefs by counsel finds as follows;

1.      That this court has jurisdiction of the subject matter and parties herein and venue in this County and District is proper.

2.      That Plaintiff's burden of proof of showing by clear, convincing and cogent evidence that a constructive trust should be imposed on certain funds has not been met.

3.      That the Court's memorandum opinion is incorporated herein by reference.

4.      That Plaintiff's Complaint is hereby dismissed with prejudice

5.      That each party will pay their own attorney fees and costs.

IT IS SO ORDERED.

_____
JAMES O. COX
SEBASTIAN COUNTY CIRCUIT JUDGE

# CHAPTER SEVEN

## The Appeal

To say I was devastated by Judge Cox's ruling is an understatement. I thought that if there was not enough proof given to demonstrate a mistake had been made, what could one ever do to convince the judge? Justice is not being served in my eyes but somehow I still felt our case was strong and now that Troy fully backed the simple premise "that a mistake had been made" we would prevail with the truth in the long run.

On April 2, 2009, I replied.

Troy:

I am sorry that the judge ruled against us. I was afraid that we would have to appeal his decision and have already been thinking about a response if, indeed, an appeal was required. Yes, we definitely want to appeal the decision. I have not yet received the judge's decision in the mail but I am familiar with your Post Trial Brief and feel that our case is sound. As to the point of there being fraud on the part of Summit, I believe that there was. I do not believe that Donna Young was an active participant with Summit; however, I do believe that Summit, with a submissive Donna Young, intentionally delayed the processing of my account to push any court action past the three-year statute concerning an error in the account records. Why otherwise, would they have taken so much time to decide the question of the TOD? What they at first did unknowingly, but very effectively accomplished, was to keep a bookkeeping error away from my Uncle Humpy so he was not able to correct it while still alive. Summit and Delta then hid the error for an additional four months, thus allowing them to escape their liability. This looks very suspicious to me and if not fraudulent, at the very least is unconscionable from the standpoint of being truthful.

My case for Fraud is as follows:

1. I notified Donna that I wished to have the bond cashed within about two weeks after Humpy's death which took place on February 24, 2004. She asked for a copy of the death certificate, which I already had asked Sue Rose to mail to me, so I was able to mail it to Donna immediately. (I wonder why she did not get one from Lois, who must have needed one to cash her bond in? Would she not already have this in her files?) Donna then sent me the forms to open an account and I signed these papers on March 25 and returned them to her. She then told me that the bond was trading below par and that if I waited for the next anniversary it could be traded in at par. I asked when that date was and she said that it was in April, so I said, "Let's wait for that and cash it in then." I do not recall that Donna ever called me back but I did call her several times. When I did next talk to Donna she told me that she had not been able to get all of the paperwork done and we had missed the anniversary date which I then found out was the 21st of April. We had almost a month to make the deadline but somehow Donna had missed it. Donna said that the next anniversary date would be October so I agreed to wait until then. I had not yet received any paperwork from her confirming my ownership nor the exact value of the account so I had to pressure her to finally receive the account documents which I then gave to you. I did not receive these until after July 10th, which is the date on them showing when they were copied. The point of all this is that I was really getting a run around and I believe that it should be obvious that the problem with the two conflicting TOD's was already known. Why was I lied to for almost four months? Is this not the definition of fraud?

Webster defines fraud by doing something by "deceit or trickery." How does a lawyer define it?

2. The three-year statute of limitations ran out on July 21st, 2007, three years to the day after the change in TOD form was mistakenly made on July 21, 2004. Donna Young never contacted me at any time through this entire period indicating that any change had been made. She did not contact me because she never realized that there was any conflict with the papers filed until the Summit lawyers told her that there was a problem when we attempted to redeem the bond in April of 2007. I found out about the decision changing the account's TOD by receiving a copy of the August 28 letter sent from Summit to Lois. This letter was conveniently written one month after the statute of limitations had passed. Perhaps it is difficult to prove fraud on this basis, but the entire timeline and actions of the people involved speaks volumes toward the suspicion that they knew very well what they were doing in delaying payment. They were trying to protect themselves from a double payout which could result from some very sloppy paper work. When I first talked to Donna Young she said the reason for the change in TOD was because the signature of Lois, naming me TOD in January of 2004, had not been properly notarized as required by law and therefore the bond had to go to Humpy's wife. That statement was not true because a notarized signature of the wife was not required, but Mr. Hill continued to use this same untrue reasoning in his deposition, and unfortunately was never challenged on the subject at that time. Their story was then changed to one where there seemed to be two TODs on the same account? There was a lot of scrambling to arrive at the final story and it had obviously started a long time before we were ever privileged with any information by receiving actual documents on the TOD.

3. I guess that this is all moot unless we are willing to take on Summit. Can that be done? They really are the ones that are responsible for this entire mess. Lois is simply the opportunistic recipient of a windfall.

Back to your initial question of appealing the decision. Yes, Troy by all means do it. Let me know the payment schedule and I will send you some retainer fees. Thanks for your counsel in this case.

On **April 3, 2009**, Troy responded.

Terry:

I have started work on the notice of appeal this morning. We have 30 days after the Judge's order was issued. We need a trial transcript. I estimate the cost of that at $2,000. Once the court reporter issues me her bill it has to be paid immediately.

We cannot go after Summit. The date of Summit's wrongful act would have been 2004 and there is a three-year statute of limitations on any fraud, negligence, or other cause of action that we would have against them.

I thought to myself, "Well, thanks Troy." This is what you have been saying, "that there is a statute of limitations of three years." So, what I have been saying is, "What happens when you just purposely push off revealing information to get past the three-year statute?" Is it not fraudulent to purposely run the time out? This fraud is not three years old, it is now! I still have to think what Summit was doing was illegal. I concluded that Troy was just not up for tangling with Summit.

On April 24, 2009 Attorney for Lois, Roy Gean Jr., wrote to Mr. Michael Hill of Summit. I did not receive a copy of this until way later, almost a month after it was written.

Dear Mr. Hill,

I am writing you for the purpose of securing the monies in the above account 8136, for Lois Druyvesteyn. I have attached a copy of your letter dated August 28, 2007 addressed to Lois Druyvesteyn in regard to this account.

On October 24, 2007 there was a Complaint for Constructive Trust and /or Declaratory Judgment filed in the Circuit Court of the Fort Smith District of Sebastian County, Arkansas by a man whose name is Terry Druyvestein. This Terry Druyvestein was the nephew of a man known as H. J. Druyvesteyn who owned the above mentioned account and which you were administering.

The Judge in this case, James O Cox, in his final Order of March 26, 2009, dismissed the Complaint with prejudice. This dismissal of the Complaint filed by Terry Druyvestein is such that Lois Druyvesteyn is now entitled to all of the sums on deposit or held in said account number 8136.

To Stay the Judgment or decision of this Court there would be no Stay given by the Court until the said Plaintiff, whose Complaint was dismissed, would file a supersedeas bond. A supersedeas bond under Arkansas law must be filed with the approval of the Court and would have sufficient financial strength so as to provide for twice the amount of that which is involved in the case, it would have to be supported by collateral or the signature of some bonding company. In this case there has been no supersedeas bond filed. I have asked Troy Gaston, the attorney for the Plaintiff, if they were contemplating the filing of a supersedeas bond. He has told me that he was not in a position to file a supersedeas bond. If Terry Druyvestein would request a Motion for Stay, it would have to be filed and all attorneys would be given a copy of such Motion and the other attorneys would then have ten days to object; and, the Court would not enter a Stay until after a hearing.

Therefore, according to the law and Arkansas Rules of Civil Procedure, the decision of the Court can be enforced. That is, the account number 8136 can be paid over to the one that the records of Summit Brokerage Services record as being the one to whom the deliverance of said monies would be in accordance to the transfer on death direction.

The main purpose of this letter, after explaining the situation that now exists so far as this litigation is concerned, is concluded by my request, as attorney for Lois Druyvesteyn, to have sent to me the documentation or papers necessary for her to execute collection of these monies. I will see that the same are secured and completed.

Sincerely,

Roy Gean, Jr.

I was shocked to receive a copy of Roy Gean's letter. In fact, it was almost a month after Roy's letter was dated that I received a copy of an email correspondence between Summit and my attorney which released my claim to account 8136 that I found out about what was happening. When I talked to Troy about it, he said that supersedeas bonds were expensive and he did not think it worth the expense. Well, that should be my decision to make! Not Troy on his own! One of the main problems with attorneys is their tendency to make decisions for you, which are of course, not always in your best interest. Troy should have made a copy of Roy's letter and sent it to me immediately, as soon as he received it. I would have looked into the cost for a bond and I would have decided if it was worth it. It would appear that Troy did not have as much confidence in an appeal as I had, or he was too pressed for time and did not want to fool with it. The main cost would have been Lois's attorney's fees if we lost our appeal, and what cost could possibly be awarded to the attorney of the appellee? Her attorney does not have much to do. (Perhaps that was a stupid statement but it seemed like we were having to do all the paperwork for the appeal.) Another cost could be interest lost as they could argue that the 2% which the fund was drawing at Summit could have been beat with some other investment. But all of these expenses combined could not be that great. Perhaps the cost of the bond company would be the greatest thing involved. We will never know because I never was given the opportunity to find out. What I did know at this point is that the money was no longer in my hands and with no control my comfort level was severely reduced.

I corresponded with Troy and told him I did not like being left out of the loop. I also told him I needed copies of the correspondence which had been going on when I was out of the loop. It also was my understanding that we would need a copy of the transcript of our initial trial for the appeal. It had to be paid as soon as it was completed. I have seen no bill.

I also did not have a copy of the appeal so what is happening?

Troy emailed back on **June 21, 2009.**

He was sorry for ignoring me. He will get me copies of the notice of appeal. They had not billed me for the transcript because it was not completed by the court reporter yet. He may have to ask for an extension for the appeal if the transcript is not ready soon. Extensions are always granted. That is the good news; the bad news is that it will add another month to six weeks before we get a decision.

I emailed Troy on **Dec. 15, 2009.**

Troy:

It has been almost six months since we last talked. I hope you are doing well with your health issues. I received the documents concerning Mr. Egan's argument in our appeal of the Lois Druyvesteyn law suite. His argument is based mostly on the decision of Mr. Hill to change the beneficiary of account No. 8136 to Lois at a time after my uncle passed away and could no longer challenge or correct a clear error. A big point in his argument is based on clear and convincing evidence. To me it is very "clear", but of course I am not the one who needs to be "convinced." I know it is hard to clearly show the error; however, Mr. Hill and Mr. Gean both chose to ignore many very important points which we have gone over many times.

(I then reiterated some of the best arguments I used before.)

I could go on and on about this, but I am afraid you may be getting as tired of the repetition as I am. Please email me your anticipated schedule for our case.

Troy emailed me back on Dec. 15, 2009.

Terry:

Yes, I agree with you. Tomorrow I am sending my reply brief which will point out the same arguments you are making. As usual, Mr. Gean was light on law. At this stage I am only allowed to write in reply to what he said. So, my next brief will be fairly short. After it is received by the court, we should hear their decision in something like four to six months.

Four to six months. How discouraging that is. And as with the legal system four to six is always eight to ten. At least that always seems to be my experience. I was to be surprised, however; it was six months when the appeals court ruled.

Cite as 2010 Ark. App. 500  *June 16, 2010*

# ARKANSAS COURT OF APPEALS

DIVISION III
**No.** CA 09-921

| | |
|---|---|
| TERRY DRUYVESTEIN<br>APPELLANT | **Opinion Delivered** June 16, 2010 |
| V. | APPEAL FROM THE SEBASTIAN<br>COUNTY CIRCUIT COURT<br>[NO. CIV-07-1383] |
| SUMMIT BROKERAGE SERVICES,<br>INC. and LOIS DRUYVESTEIN<br>APPELLEES | HONORABLE JAMES O. COX,<br>JUDGE |
| | REVERSED AND REMANDED |

**COURTNEY HUDSON HENRY, Judge**

Appellant Terry Druyvestein appeals the order entered by the Circuit Court of Sebastian County dismissing his complaint that sought the creation of a constructive trust. For reversal, appellant contends that the circuit court's decision is clearly erroneous. We find merit in this argument and reverse and remand.

The record reflects that H.J. "Humpy" Druyvestein died on February 24, 2007, survived by his wife, appellee Lois Druyvestein. Appellant is the son of Humpy's deceased brother. During his life, Humpy held two bond accounts at Morgan Stanley that were managed by his broker, Donna Young. One account was payable at Humpy's death to appellant, while the other was payable upon his death to the daughter of his second wife, Sue Rose, and her son, John Rose. In early January 2004, Young left Morgan Stanley and moved to a firm called Delta Financial, where she operated as a broker for appellee Summit.

Cite as 2010 Ark. App. 500

Brokerage Services, Inc. (Summit). Humpy transferred the two bond accounts from Morgan Stanley to Delta Financial on January 28, 2004. In so doing, Humpy executed a registration application for an account ending in the number 8136, designating appellant as the beneficiary of the account upon Humpy's death. Humpy completed a similar document for an account ending in the number 8134, naming Lois as the death beneficiary of that account.

In July 2004, Humpy executed a registration application that changed the transfer-on-death designation of the 8136 account to Lois. However, until months after Humpy's death, the 8136 account remained entitled "H.J. Druyvestein TOD Terry Druyvestein." According to Young, even though her signature appeared on the document changing the beneficiary of the 8136 account to Lois, she was oblivious to the alteration, and, when Humpy died, she advised both Lois and appellant to wait until October 2007 to liquidate the accounts in order to receive full par value. Lois did not accept that advice and cashed in the 8134 account in April 2007. Appellant intended to heed Young's advice, and Young established an account for him to receive the funds in October. However, Summit dishonored the request to transfer the funds in the 8136 account to appellant after discovering the July 2004 registration application that named Lois as the transfer-on-death beneficiary. On August 28, 2007, Michael Hill, an executive vice president and the chief compliance officer at Summit, wrote Lois a letter stating that the 8136 account should have been changed to reflect her name as the transfer-on-death beneficiary as of July 2004 and that steps were being taken to accomplish that correction.

Cite as 2010 Ark. App. 500

On October 24, 2007, appellant filed suit against Summit and Lois seeking to establish a constructive trust in the 8136 account. As a result of the litigation, Summit froze the account. Later, the parties proposed and the circuit court entered an agreed order dismissing Summit from the lawsuit with prejudice. The case proceeded to trial against Lois, who was unable to attend due to poor health.

In his testimony, appellant stated that his father and Humpy worked together and were close brothers. He said that he now lived in Montana and that he arranged a family reunion in 2002 where he met Lois, Humpy's new wife. Appellant said that Humpy called him in 2003 and said that he had a bond that he wanted to leave him when he died. He testified that they briefly discussed the bond again in July 2004 at another family reunion and that Humpy said nothing to him about removing his name from the bond. Appellant said that he visited Humpy and Lois in 2006 and that Humpy spoke of the bond and also about leaving him a chair that had belonged to his grandfather. He testified that, when Humpy left the room, Lois told him that he could thank her for putting the bond in his name.

Appellant testified that he spoke to Lois after Humpy's funeral and that she asked him if he had cashed the bond. He said that Lois advised him to get the money before John Rose did. Appellant stated that he decided to wait until October 2007 to cash the bond in order to receive full value. He said that he learned that there was a problem in September 2007 when he received a letter stating that Lois's name was on the final TOD form. Appellant testified that he telephoned Lois and spoke to her daughter, Linda Van Divner, because Lois

-3- CA 09-921

was in the hospital. He said that Linda told him that Summit must have made a mistake. Appellant called Linda a few weeks later, and she referred him to Lois's attorney.

Appellant testified that Humpy's intentions were clear and that he must have signed the July 2004 TOD form by mistake. He said that Humpy could not have realized that his name had been removed from the account because he had talked to Humpy many times since the change occurred.

Loretta Druyvestein, appellant's wife, testified that she was a witness to the conversation between Humpy and appellant about the bond at the reunion in July 2004. She said that Lois did not contradict Humpy's statements that he wanted appellant to have the bond. Loretta testified that she spoke with Linda after the mistake was discovered and that Linda acknowledged that the bond was supposed to go to appellant. She also recalled the visit in 2006 when Humpy spoke about the bond at the kitchen table.

Young testified that she had serviced Humpy's accounts since 1998 and that from 2004 to 2007 she met with Humpy and Lois at least four times a year. She said that Lois was present when the accounts were transferred in January 2004 when Humpy made his wishes known that he wanted to keep appellant as the death beneficiary on the one account and that he wanted Lois to be the death beneficiary on the other account, instead of Sue and John Rose. Young testified that Humpy never indicated that he wanted appellant removed as the death beneficiary and that it was always her understanding, Humpy's understanding, and Lois's understanding that appellant was to receive the 8136 account at Humpy's death. She said that

-4-                                                            CA 09-921

Cite as 2010 Ark. App. 500

Humpy received separate monthly statements on both accounts and that one would have been titled "H.J. Druyvestein TOD Terry Druyvestein," while the other would have read "H.J. Druyvestein TOD Lois Druyvestein." Young stated that the designations would have been obvious to anyone who would have viewed the envelope. She testified that, in the many meetings she had with Humpy and Lois after July 2004, Lois never questioned why appellant's name still appeared on the account. Young stated that, when Lois contacted her about Humpy's death, Lois did not inquire about the 8136 account and that Lois never asked why she was not receiving the monthly statements regarding the 8136 account following Humpy's death.

Young further testified that Humpy did not ask her to change the death beneficiary on the account in July 2004. She said that she had no doubt whatsoever that Humpy never wanted to remove appellant from the 8136 account. Young said that, if Humpy had asked her to change the beneficiary to Lois, she would have simply moved the assets from the 8136 account to Lois's 8134 account rather than have Humpy execute a change in beneficiary form. Young asserted that the execution of the form was a mistake. She said that, had the title of the account been changed as it should have been when the form was completed, then both she and Humpy would have been alerted about the mistake and that it could have been corrected. She had no recollection as to why the change in beneficiary form was executed. Her best explanation was that it was a housekeeping matter requested by the home office. She explained that, when the accounts were moved from Morgan Stanley to Delta Financial,

-5-                                                      CA 09-921

Cite as 2010 Ark. App. 500

the 8134 account should have been registered the same way as it was previously titled in the names of Sue and John Rose and then changed to designate Lois as the beneficiary. Young thought that the change in beneficiary form was perhaps executed to correct that oversight. She also surmised that she may have written the wrong account number on the form.

John Rose testified that Humpy conveyed most of his property, including Humpy's home, to him and his mother and that he managed other properties for Humpy. He said that Humpy told him that he intended for appellant to have the bond when he died. Rose stated that Humpy left Lois two duplexes in addition to the one bond account. Karen Spring, Humpy's niece and appellant's sister, testified that Lois called her in the summer of 2007 with complaints about John Rose. Spring said that Lois acknowledged that appellant was to receive the bond and that Lois assumed that he would share it with his siblings.

Michael Hill testified by deposition that he reviews all transfers in excess of $100,000 and that the discrepancy between the 8136 account title and the July 2004 change in beneficiary was discovered when appellant made the request to transfer the assets in the account. He said that, based on the July 2004 document, Summit recognized Lois as the beneficiary of the 8136 account. Hill testified that Lois did not claim the 8136 account because he did not think that she knew that she was the beneficiary of another account. He stated that, when he spoke with Young, she seemed surprised about the change in beneficiary and that she said that the beneficiary should have been appellant. The final witness, Linda

-6-                                                                 CA 09-921

Van Divner, testified that Humpy never said anything to her about the bond. She denied ever speaking to Loretta.

The circuit court took the case under advisement and later issued a letter opinion outlining the testimony and evidence and setting forth its decision. In its ruling, the court stated that Young confessed to making an egregious mistake but found that her testimony was confusing because she could not specifically recall what occurred on the day that Humpy changed the death beneficiary from appellant to Lois. The circuit court also noted that, after the change was made, Humpy met with Young at least four times a year but that no further changes were made to the account. Citing as analogous the decision in *Trimble v. Trimble*, 181 Ark. 350, 25 S.W.2d 758 (1930), the circuit court determined that, based on the evidence, it could find no clear and convincing evidence of a mistake. Therefore, the court denied appellant's request to establish a constructive trust.

Appellant argues on appeal that the evidence supported a finding that the change in beneficiary form was executed by mistake and that the circuit court's refusal to impose a constructive trust is clearly erroneous. A constructive trust is an implied trust that arises by operation of law when equity demands. *Waterall v. Waterall*, 85 Ark. App. 363, 155 S.W.3d 30 (2004). It is imposed where a person holding title to property is subject to an equitable duty to convey it to another on the ground that he would be unjustly enriched if he were permitted to retain it. *Tripp v. Miller*, 82 Ark. App. 236, 105 S.W.3d 804 (2003). The duty to convey the property may arise because it was conveyed through fraud, duress, undue

-7- CA 09-921

Cite as 2010 Ark. App. 500

influence or mistake, breach of fiduciary duty, or wrongful disposition of another's property. *Id.* To impose a constructive trust, there must be full, clear, and convincing evidence leaving no doubt as to the necessary facts. *Higgins v. Higgins*, 2010 Ark. App. 71, ___ S.W.3d ___.

Although we review traditional equity cases de novo, the test on review is not whether we are convinced that there is clear and convincing evidence to support the circuit court's findings but whether we can say that the circuit court's findings are clearly erroneous. *Statler v. Painter*, 84 Ark. App. 114, 133 S.W.3d 425 (2003). A finding is clearly erroneous when, although there is evidence to support it, the reviewing court on the entire evidence is left with a definite and firm conviction that a mistake was made. *McCracken v. McCracken*, 2009 Ark. App. 758, ___ S.W.3d ___.

We are left with a definite and firm conviction that the circuit court was mistaken in its decision. All witnesses who professed knowledge of Humpy's wishes testified that Humpy intended to leave the account to appellant. If that were the sum total of the evidence, we could have no quarrel with the circuit court's decision, as the court was entitled to make its own assessment of the witnesses' credibility. However, the testimony was strongly corroborated by objective facts that compel a conclusion that the change in beneficiary form was executed by mistake. It is undisputed that, after the document was executed in July 2004, the account title continued to reflect that appellant was the designated beneficiary of the account upon Humpy's death. It is also without dispute that Humpy received monthly statements showing appellant as the beneficiary of the account. Humpy, apparently a seasoned

-8-                                                                                    CA 09-921

Cite as 2010 Ark. App. 500

businessman, met quarterly with Young, and at no time did he register a complaint about appellant remaining as the death beneficiary in the two years and seven months preceding his death. We are also mindful that Lois attended the quarterly meetings with Young and that Lois did not lay claim to the account following Humpy's death. Although Young was at a loss to explain what happened, her testimony was unequivocal that she made a mistake and that Humpy did not ask her to remove appellant as the beneficiary of the account. Based on the record as a whole, we hold that the circuit court's ruling is clearly erroneous.

Also, we have studied the case the circuit court relied upon and conclude that it is not particularly germane to the issue presented in this appeal. In *Trimble, supra,* Trimble spoke often about changing the beneficiary of his life insurance policy. However, he never took the steps necessary to accomplish that goal, and the supreme court affirmed the chancellor's refusal to grant reformation. Here, the owner of the account did execute a form changing the beneficiary designation of an account, and the question is whether the owner intended to do so or whether it was accomplished by mistake. Thus, the issues in the two cases are quite different. Consequently, *Trimble* is not persuasive authority.

Reversed and remanded.

ROBBINS and GRUBER, JJ., agree.

# CHAPTER EIGHT

## We Won – or Not!

I emailed Troy on June 17, 2010, at 9:59 AM.

Troy:

Y ou certainly were the bearer of good news yesterday. Thank you for your diligent work on what turned out to be a long ordeal. I am uncertain as to how things will proceed. Will Judge Cox now change his order and create the trust? Will he be involved in getting the funds back? If you can give me a general idea of what to expect and how we must now proceed, it will be helpful to me. Are we now supposed to proceed with notification of Lois and her attorney or will Judge Cox do this? Anyway, thanks again for your good work.

I was ecstatic! Finally, this long battle was over and justice had prevailed. The hours of work and laying awake nights thinking about how this wrong could be set right were over. When one puts the time and effort into a case like this where the outcome is anything but certain, it is as if a large load is taken from your back and you are grateful. There would be a celebration tonight.

Troy emailed me back on June 17, 2010, at 10:06 AM.

Terry:

Judge Cox has already set a hearing to order Lois or the daughter to put the funds into the registry of the court. I have sent notice of that hearing to Roy Gean on behalf of Lois.

Once the court has your money, I will then prepare paperwork for the court to pay the money to you.The hearing is set for July 1st and I will be appearing in court for you on that day.You do not have to be there but you are of course welcome.No testimony will be taken unless I am questioning Linda about where the assets are located if she does not produce them before that time.

Thank you for the kind words.I was elated to get the news. Congratulations.

I emailed Troy on June 21, 2010, 9:32 AM

Troy:

Thanks Troy, for the update.We will be looking forward to the July 1st hearing.Of course we would like you to represent us.

Troy emailed me on June 21, 2010, 12:50 PM

Terry:

Bad news.Lois has appealed the decision from the Arkansas Court of Appeal to the Supreme Court of Arkansas.I will tell you that I am 99% certain that we will win at this level.The bad news is that it will probably delay the July 1st hearing another month or six weeks.I will represent you at the Supreme Court.It will not require a hearing and will primarily involve us re-submitting the same briefs plus me pointing out that the Court of Appeal ruled for us.

Another bonus – the Justice who wrote your Appeal decision was Courtney Henry.She just won a statewide election to the Supreme Court.

Well, it could not hurt our case – having the appeal court's writer now on the Supreme Court.The only problem, as Troy pointed out, is that this just goes on and on.I think the appeal to the Supreme Court is just a delay tactic.But a delay for what purpose?It could also be a delay because we are up against a shady attorney to say the least and he may have lots of time to file appeals.We shall see.

In July Troy prepared our response to the Petition for Review which had been submitted by Lois and her attorney to the Arkansas Supreme Court.

**ARGUMENT**:

The only argument Appellant would make in reply to the Appellee's Brief is to note clear flaws in the logic of the Appellee's Brief. The Appellee argues that because there was a Change of Beneficiary Form as to account number 8136 that this form controls.

But, it is clear that this Change of Beneficiary Form was completed by mistake. Donna Young testified that she originally opened these accounts at Morgan Stanley and that Sue Rose was the beneficiary on account 8134 and Terry Druyvestein was the beneficiary on account 8136. The original applications opening these accounts with Summit Brokerage, once Donna Young had moved from Morgan Stanley to Summit, both are clearly checked as original applications and dated January 28, 2004. Lois Druyvesteyn was incorrectly listed as the original beneficiary on account 8134 even though Sue Rose had been on this account at Morgan Stanley. The only error, at this point, is that Lois Druyvesteyn was listed as the original owner when a Change of Beneficiary Form should have been filled out when the account moved from Morgan Stanley to Delta. Donna Young then testified that it is most probable that there was later a mistake made in putting account number 8136 on a Change of Beneficiary Form when it was intended to be for account number 8134.

In other words, there was a mistake made because account 8134 is the one that needed to be changed because it had to be brought over from Morgan Stanley exactly as it was – with the TOD recorded under Sue Rose's name. That was not done on January 28, 2004 so it was corrected in July of that year. Only problem was, Donna Young made a mistake on the account numbers. Donna Young testified there was never any intention by H. J. Druyvesteyn to change the beneficiary on account 8136.

There was absolutely no evidence to dispute the testimony of Donna Young that there was clearly a mistake made. The only evidence introduced to dispute Donna Young's testimony was the document signed by H. J. Druyvesteyn. But this document was created by Donna Young and she is the only person who testified who had personal knowledge of its creation. She testified that when it was created that H. J. Druyvesteyn had no intention to remove Terry Druyvestein from his account and he expressed as much to her.

-Troy Gaston

Well, Troy was now right on the mark. I could tell he clearly understood the facts and could see how the mistake was made. I wished that we could have just as clearly presented this to Judge Cox in the initial trial. I must say that this had all become much clearer as the trial progressed and the appeals court had clearly filled in the many pieces to the puzzle. What I had tried to express to Judge Cox was perhaps too much in the form of a theory and was not paid much attention to. Where we missed the boat was not following this up more logically and clearly with the testimony of our witnesses. Particularly that of Donna Young, who in Judge Cox's own words, called her testimony founded on "supposition, guesses and assumptions." I believe that Troy was too focused on the "undue influence" theory too long and did not have the time left before trial to fully develop what really had happened. I don't blame him too much for this as all of Humpy's family and his close friends knew what Lois had done to control Humpy towards the end and it was not pretty. I really do not know how much she had initially cared for him, but in the last year in particular, she was in it for the money and allowed her attorney to ignore justice and replace it with greed.

On Feb. 3, 2011, the Supreme Court made their decision on Lois's appeal.

Leslie W. Steen
Clerk

Office of the Clerk
Supreme Court of the State of Arkansas
Arkansas Court of Appeals
Justice Building
625 Marshall Street
Little Rock, Arkansas 72201

February 3, 2011

Roy Gean, Jr.
Attorney at Law
511 Garrison Avenue
Fort Smith, Arkansas 72901

> RE: 10 00720
> Terry Druyvestein
> v.
> Summit Brokerage Services, Inc., et al.

Dear Mr. Gean:

The Arkansas Supreme Court issued the following order today in the above styled case:

"Petition for review is denied. Henry, J., not participating."

Sincerely,

LWS:sc
cc: Troy Gaston
 Ken Blevins, Clerk
 (No. CV-07-1383)

Leslie W. Steen, Clerk

On Feb. 4, 2011, 12:30 PM, I heard from Troy.

Terry

We won the appeal at the Supreme Court level. I have already written to the judge asking for a hearing to give us an accounting of what they did with the assets.

On Feb. 4, 2011, 3:25 PM, I replied to Troy.

Troy:

So glad to hear the good news! I know you had confidence that we would win but I was starting to have doubts. It restores my faith in the legal system. I can see that your win will have far reaching implications for cases in the future. Good work. I guess the first thing is to find out what Lois and Linda did with the money. How about Mr. Gean? Will he have to give back his percentage? I certainly hope so.

Well this was an exciting day but we have had some of these before. In fact, this entire case has been a series of roller coaster rides. I never thought it would be this hard. What I thought looked like an unintentional mistake from the beginning, has taken up thousands of man hours on both sides, not to mention the impact on all levels of the Judicial System. The best part now seemed to be vindication – finally the legal system saw through the false claims of Lois, Linda and their attorney and now justice would be served. I wondered if there was any possibility of getting attorney's fees back. By backing this from the start on an hourly basis I had a lot out on a limb. I also had doubts that it had been the best way to go. Especially after the past four years and the uncertainty of winning a case which in my mind had initially seemed like a "slam dunk." I wonder if there is anything close to a slam dunk in the "justice system."

On Feb. 7, 2011, Troy wrote to Judge Cox.
RE: Terry Druyvestein v Lois Druyvesteyn and Summit Brokerage Services
Dear Judge Cox:
The above-referenced matter has been decided by the Supreme Court of Arkansas. They have denied Mr. Gean's Petition for Review. I would ask that you set this case for a one-hour inquiry hearing and Order that Mr. Gean's client or Linda Van Divner be present to provide an accounting of the disposition of the assets that were paid out of the Registry of the Court. The court may recall that Linda came under the jurisdiction of the court when she requested and was granted permission to appear on behalf of her mother in this proceeding.

-Troy Gaston

On March 12, 2011, I exchanged emails with Troy as follows:

Troy:

Just wanted to touch base before your appearance before Judge Cox on the 18th. As mentioned before, I will not be able to appear with you. I do however have some concerns about what may take place at the hearing.

1. I have never trusted Summit Brokerage so will be interested in what they turned over to the court. I gave you a ballpark estimate of what I thought the amount should be, at least previously. This was based on the account ledger given to me by Summit after Humpy's death when Donna Young still observed me as the account owner. If we do not agree with what was turned over to the Court, can we get the Judge to order Summit to turn over the records for our review? I guess there is no reason to speculate on this until we find out what was turned over; however, I just want you to be prepared if something does not look right. **Troy's Answer: I believe that Summit turned over the correct amount. The amount was not paid in at the time of the judgment. The amount was paid in when we first sued Summit, within a few weeks of us opening the case. At that time both Lois' attorney and myself had a mutual interest in getting the maximum money from Lois. We both reviewed copies of the account statements up to the time when litigation began and agreed that the amount deposited in with the court was accurate. But, once we get our money we can re-review or re-request records to make you feel better.**

2. I do believe we should ask the Judge to award us interest. I am certain that Linda will have a sob story as to how much it costs to keep her mother but she was given lots of assets besides this bond. Troy: I agree.

3. I would assume that if the full amount is not handed over to the Court at the hearing, and if certain things need to be negotiated, such as interest, or time schedule for payment, that we will talk before reaching an agreement. Troy: **I am worried what will happen is that Linda will show up, saying that Lois is dreadfully ill, and plead ignorance. At that**

point I am going to tell the judge that my clients are not going to get screwed out of a quarter of a million dollars because she has misplaced that kind of money and ask him to order her to turn over all of hers and Lois' personal banking records within 20 days or be held in contempt and jailed.

On March 16, 2011, Judge Cox preempted the hearing set for the 18th. Dear Counselors:

This matter is set on my Friday, March 18, 2011 docket for a hearing, but in reviewing the case and the Mandate of the Arkansas Court of Appeals, I don't see that a hearing is actually necessary and I enclose an Order which I think disposes of this matter.

The simple issue at trial was whether the account involved should have been paid to Terry Druyvestein, Plaintiff or Lois Druyvesteyn, Humpy's wife. My opinion from the trial found that the money should be paid to Lois Druyvesteyn; however, the Court of Appeals has determined I was mistaken in my decision. Since there is but one alternative to my decision, it is obvious that the money should be paid to Terry Druyvestein.

Therefore, I am enclosing an Order entered this date directing a Lois Druyvesteyn to pay over the sum of money which she received, pursuant to liquidation of the account, to Terry Druyvestein with interest at the rate of 5.75% per annum from the date that she received it until paid. The money should be remitted to Mr. Druyvestein within ten days. If the money is not paid within that period of time, Mr. Druyvestein will be entitled to judgment against Lois Druyvesteyn for those sums. It is my hope that Mrs. Druyvesteyn has been a good steward of the funds and can simply remit them to Terry Druyvestein forthwith. If that is not the case and testimony is required in this matter, please contact me and I will reset this matter for hearing. I have removed the matter from Friday's docket.

TERRY DRUYVESTEIN

IN THE CIRCUIT COURT OF SEBASTIAN COUNTY, ARKANSAS
FORT SMITH DISTRICT
CIVIL DIVISION VI

TERRY DRUYVESTEIN                                              PLAINTIFF

vs.                   CASE NO. CV 2007-1383 (VI)

SUMMIT BROKERAGE                                              DEFENDANT
SERVICES, INC. and
LOIS DRUYVESTEIN

## ORDER

Now on this 16th day of March, 2011 this cause comes on for consideration upon the Mandate of the Arkansas Court of Appeals filed February 4, 2011 in these proceedings together with the Court's Opinion. From a review of the opinion and mandate the Court finds as follows:

1.     That Terry Druyvestein is entitled to the funds which where subject of the trial held in this case.

2.     That Summit Brokerage Services, Inc. paid said sums to Lois Druyvestein.

3.     That Lois Druyvestein should remit the sums at issue, which she received from Summit Brokerage Services, Inc., together with interest at the rate of 5.7% per annum from the date received to the date of payment to Terry Druyvestein.

4.     That the sums should be remitted from Ms. Druyvestein to Terry Druyvestein forthwith.

118

5.      That if the sums of money due Terry Druyvestein by Lois Druyvestein are not paid within ten (10) days of the date of entry of this order, Terry Druyvestein shall be entitled to judgment against Lois Druyvestein for said sums, and if it is necessary to determine the amount of said judgment, this matter will be set for hearing specifically to deal with the amount of the judgment to which Terry Druyvestein shall be entitled.

IT IS SO ORDERED.

_____
JAMES O. COX
SEBASTIAN COUNTY CIRCUIT JUDGE

The next day, March 17, 2011, Troy wrote to Judge Cox:

Dear Judge Cox:

I appreciate you entering Judgment in our case. I can assure you I would not have asked for the Court to set this case for hearing if I had not already spoken to Roy Gean Jr. and confirmed with him that his client is going to claim that she does not know where the money is at.

I am requesting that you set this case for hearing in Aid of Judgment because I have already had a telephone conference with Roy and he has told me that he does not have any idea where the money is and he is not even sure if he made the check out to the daughter or to the mother. He said that the mother is in some home somewhere and is not capable of participating in the trial. As such, I would like the opportunity to question the daughter at a hearing in Aid Judgment for this court to help ascertain where the funds that this court has control over are located. I know that since the time that this litigation began that certain real property has already been transferred from the mother to the daughter. The daughter's name is Linda J. Van Divner. She specifically requested from you that she be allowed to appear on behalf of her mother at the original trial. You granted that relief. As such, I believe that this court has jurisdiction over her to require her to appear for questioning.

Again, my client is looking at losing close to a quarter of a million dollars if swift action is not taken. Please set this matter for a 30-minute hearing in Aid of the Judgment that you anticipate entering. If they turn over the money, which Roy Gean has indicated that he does not even know where it is, then I will be more than happy for you to cancel the hearing.

-Troy Gaston

I emailed Troy on March 19, 2011.

Troy, what happened on the 18th?

Troy emailed back on March 21, 2011.

Terry:

I am sorry that I did not get back to you on Friday. Another trial took my time. The Judge entered an order giving Lois ten days to turn the money over to us. If she does not make any effort, we are to proceed with contempt or filing an action against her daughter.

Roy Gean to Judge Cox, March 25, 2011.
Comes now Defendant, Lois Druyvesteyn, and for her Motion for Reconsideration, alleges and states:

1. That the interest rate paid on the bond which is the subject matter of the present litigation was not 5.7 per annum and the percentage was less than the said amount on the Order of this Court.
2. Wherefore, the Defendant, Lois Druyvestein, prays the court to amend said Order of the Court to show the true interest rate that said bond would be drawing during the period of time and since the payment of the sums of money to said Defendant.

On **April 4, 2011**, Judge Cox issued the following order.

**IN THE CIRCUIT COURT OF SEBASTIAN COUNTY, ARKANSAS
FORT SMITH DISTRICT
PROBATE DIVISION**

TERRY DRUYVESTEIN                                              **PLAINTIFF**

VS.                        **CASE NO. CV-2007-1383**

SUMMIT BROKERAGE
SERVICES, INC. and
LOIS DRUYVESTEIN                                      **DEFENDANTS**

### ORDER

Comes on now for hearing an upon the courts own Motion in the above-referenced matter and the Court does grant a Judgment to the Plaintiff, Terry Druyvestein, against the Defendant, Lois Druyvestein in the amount of $200,000 plus 2% per annum back to the date of the original Judgment entered by this court.

1. Lois Druyvestein was served with Post Judgment Interrogatories by attorney Troy Gaston in this matter by service of the same upon her attorney Roy Gean. She is given 10 days from the date of this Order to answer such Post Judgment Interrogatories which have been served more than forty (40) days in the past. Failure to answer such Post Judgment Interrogatories may result in an Order of Contempt.

**IT IS SO ORDERED.**

_____
Honorable James O. Cox
Circuit Judge

Date: 4-4-11

TG:dd

122

I can hardly catch my breath. Things keep happening, threats of Contempt, Orders, Changes to orders, promises. It appears that a lot is happening but is it? I think it is time for a little less talk and a lot more action. I have often been told that we are a Country of Law. In other words, we function because of our conviction to obey the law. Well what happens if one does not obey the law? They say one can stay out of jail almost indefinitely with the aid of a good attorney. I think that must be true. Just look at the people on death row who have been there for 20 years. But then death is a serious matter and I make no judgments with respect to the death penalty. I do believe more money is spent in attempting to enforce the death penalty than what would be spent on keeping the prisoner for the remainder of his life. So from a financial standpoint, the death penalty is poor policy. On the other hand, I have read about some crimes so heinous that the animal who committed them doesn't deserve to live either. I guess I will leave these heavy questions in the hands of God. But the point is, what if we as a society choose not to obey the law and the decisions of our courts? Will we all be put in jail? No, we would just have anarchy and a collapse of our country.

Now, let's take just a few cases in which people choose not to obey the laws and orders of the courts. I think it happens a lot and there is a fine line between observing and actually obeying the laws of our land. The threat of jail time is real as long as we do not have to put too many into jail. If laws are unfair, as was the case with the Whiskey Tax in the 1790s, people revolt and civil war is possible. So our judicial system has to be seen as fair or we stand to collapse as a nation. Right now there is great strife because people of color believe that they are often unjustly targeted by the police. This perception is often fueled by politicians and the news media. Our legal system must remain above reproach if we are to survive as a nation. I submit that we must be on guard to insure that justice is done and not that the person with the best attorney wins. The place where that must be observed is in our courtrooms and with the practice of law. The first defense of our legal system lies with the ethics practiced by the legal profession itself.

# CHAPTER NINE
## The Collection

I have some bad news to report. Sue Rose has passed away. She had been struggling with respiratory issues for some time and her body could no longer handle the stress of it I guess. Anyway she will be missed and I wish she could have seen the end of this case, but then the end is not yet in sight. I can say that she helped me a lot in recovering things which I may not have gotten back from Lois if not for her assistance. I regret that her family lost the relationship with Humpy because of the selfishness of Lois. I am a blood relative but Bob, Sue and Jon Rose were the closest thing to family that Humpy had.

I emailed Troy on April 14, 2011.

Troy:

I understood Judge Cox to give Lois 10 days to appear after his order of April 4. Did anything happen? This is ten days.

Troy answered April 15, 2011.

Terry:

Only that Roy has told me and the court that he dropped the ball on the questions that I had sent him. I had to resend them to him. He has promised me and the court we will have the responses within 10 days and also that we will get an offer to pay cash now. I am asking the Judge to set a hearing for the following week so if Roy doesn't come through on his promise we can move more quickly.

I read that as they are going to try and settle. I am looking into Kansas counsel for you. If their offer is not a good one, then I think you should proceed with registering your judgment in Kansas so you can put a lien on her home. I talked to Donna Young who told me Lois bought a new home in Kansas soon after our original case.

OK, so the judge gives the attorney ten days and then gives him another ten days because he "dropped the ball?" I can just see that happening if I had defied the judge's orders. Fact is, this attorney for Lois has constantly stalled. It is four years and we get a judgment and my attorney thinks they are going to give us a settlement offer? I thought you made settlement offers before the trial, in an attempt to avoid the expense and uncertainty of a trial. Now we finally get a judgment and my attorney is talking settlement? He is also talking about getting a Kansas attorney so I can file my judgment against Lois there! Does this court no longer have any jurisdiction? Was not the crime committed in Arkansas and can't the judge order her back to make restitution? I have even heard of cases where people from "out of state" were called back to pay parking fines or is that just rumor? Anyway, I am thinking this is just not right. The extra ten days the judge gave Roy passes and nothing happens.

ON APRIL 26, 2011,

### IN THE CIRCUIT COURT OF SEBASTIAN COUNTY, ARKANSAS CASE NO. CV-2007-1383

Terry Druyvestein, Plaintiff    V.    Lois Druyvesteyn, Defendant

### ORDER TO PERMIT DAUGHTER OF LOIS DRUYVESTEYN TO ANSWER THE INTERROGATORIES

On this 26th day of April, 2011, comes before this Court the Defendant's Motion filed by her daughter, Linda Van Divner, to answer the interrogatories, and the court finding good cause for said Motion enters the following Order:

IT IS, THEREFORE, ORDERED ADJUDGED AND DECREED that the Defendant is allowed a period of time to May 13, 2011, to Answer said Interrogatories and Request for Production of Documents by submitting a copy of said Answers and Responses to the attorney of record for the Plaintiff as well as a copy to the Court.

AND, IT IS SO ORDERED    CIRCUIT JUDGE, JAMES O. COX

OK, so let Linda answer the questions. It's OK with me, let's get on with it.

On May 2, 2011, I email Troy.

Troy:

This case just seems to linger on with never any satisfaction. Why have we not been able to even get Lois or Linda before the judge? It is hard to understand how they can continue to stall in this matter. If they do not respond, why doesn't Judge Cox just hold them in contempt and allow us to go after any assets she has? At this point I still do not have any papers showing how much was in Humpy's account when it was turned over to Lois, much less any accrued interest to argue about. I also wonder why or how we allowed Mr. Gean to get his hands on it in the first place. Also, why does Mr. Gean seem to keep the contingency fee he received before actually "losing" the case? Don't attorneys only get to keep a contingency fee when they win the case? My uncle gave Lois the two duplexes in Barling at the same time he passed the Ford Motor Company bond to me and my family. Now Lois has both and has slipped the assets to her daughter. Do we now have to sue Linda? In Kansas? Doesn't Judge Cox see through this? (Or is Judge Cox part of the problem? Him and his favorite attorney, Roy Gean?) Why doesn't Judge Cox let us go after the duplexes and if the value is there, forget about the Kansas property? I am really getting impatient in this matter.

On **May 3, 2011**, Troy replied.

Terry:

I agree that this case seems to go on and on. Getting a reversal on appeal over cash that has already been spent puts people in this situation. It is a shame the judge did not listen to me at the original hearing and we would not be dealing with this. I have now sent two letters and filed a motion for contempt and also met with the judge to ask him to hurry up and hold them in contempt.

The time has passed for them to give us answers and I have filed a Motion for Contempt against Lois. I will forward that to you in a separate email in just a moment. I mailed it to you previously as well. It should have been there by now.

I have also asked the judge to order Linda to appear in court since she did so at trial. He has given Linda until May 13th to answer the same questions. I have been complaining about this since they were due at the end of March. They are the post-judgment interrogatories. I am as frustrated as you are about the lack of urgency with which the court has treated our case. Mr. Gean is telling him that they are going to offer us a cash settlement and the money is there. I think Mr. Gean is just trying to buy more and more time.

The amount that was given to Lois is the amount that was in the registry of the Court. The court clerk will have a record of that exact figure. I can get that document from her. I believed that it was only $200,000 or very near that because the account did not pay any interest due to the fact that Summit gave it to the Court almost four years ago.

You asked how we "allowed" them to get their hands on the money. We did not allow anything. Once you lose a case at the trial level the opposing party is entitled by law to take possession of the money unless you post a cash bond. A judgment in circuit court is final and when the money is in the registry of the court it gets distributed to the prevailing party automatically. We did not agree to allow them to do that. The judge's mistake in ruling against us at trial meant that we had to come up with $200,000 cash to post a bond or that Lois would get the money pending appeal.

Roy denies that he was paid any portion of the funds and that he was paid in advance out of the money that Lois got from her own TOD account. It is true that Roy does normally work on an advanced retainer. But, the discovery I have sent to Lois covers where all of the money went and will tell us whether it was paid to Roy. If part of it was paid to Roy, I will ask the court to order it returned. We will get copies of the checks written.

We have filed a lien against the duplexes already. They cannot be sold without your signature. So if we do not get cash from Lois, then we can go about forcing a sale of the duplexes. That will be my next step in Arkansas. I would still advise registering the judgment in Kansas which will then create a lien against Lois' home. Donna Young has told me that Lois purchased a new home while the case was on appeal. If you take all of the real estate together there should be sufficient assets to collect on the judgment in your favor.

The good news is that Lois and Linda do have assets. A lot of people in your situation find that their money was spent at the casino or on luxury items and there are no assets to go after. I do believe you will get paid sooner or later.

-Troy Gaston

Roy Gean had until **May 13, 2011** to get answers to the interrogatories Troy had requested and had been actually due for over a month. Finally, on May 13th, they were received, if you could actually call them that.

## LOIS DRUYVESTEYN'S RESPONSES TO PLAINTIFF'S FIRST INTERROGATORIES AND REQUEST FOR PRODUCTION OF DOCUMENTS

Comes now Defendant, Lois Druyvesteyn, by her Durable Power of Attorney, Linda Van Divner and responses to Plaintiff 's First Interrogatories and Request for Production of Documents as follows:

INTERROGATORY NO. 1: Please provide the account where the funds that were transferred to Lois Druyvesteyn as a result of this litigation are currently located including the name of the institution, the type of account, and the account number.

ANSWER: The funds were not placed into an account to my knowledge. The funds were received in the form of a check and Defendant Druyvesteyn endorsed the check and her attorney cashed it. The funds have been spent on Defendant Druyvesteyn's legal fees, medical expenses and living expenses.

INTERROGATORY NO. 2: Please describe any transfers that have been made from Lois Druyvesteyn to Linda J. Van Divner since the inception of this matter.

ANSWER: None. The subject of this litigation is not a transfer. All funds received have been spent on Defendant Druyvesteyn's expenses.

INTERROGATORY NO. 3: Please provide a list of all debts which are currently owed by Lois Druyvesteyn or which have been paid by or on behalf of Lois Druyvesteyn since the original judgment was entered by the trial court in this case.

ANSWER: Legal fees in the amount of approximately $108,000, monthly living expenses for assisted living care ranging from $3,800 to $4,200 per month, supplemental health insurance premiums of $541 per month and life insurance premiums of $47 per month.

INTERROGATORY NO. 4: Please provide a list of all checking accounts in the name of Lois Druyvesteyn.

ANSWER: Marshall and Isley Bank, Account No. 42051306. PROVIDE DOCUMENTS: A bank statement ending November 4, 2010 (one year ago) was provided showing a balance of $1,133.

INTERROGATORY NO. 5: Please provide the name of the institution, bank account number, and the names on the account where the funds from the subject account were placed following judgment.

ANSWER: When originally received the funds were received in the form of a check. Defendant Lois Druyvesteyn endorsed the check and gave it to her attorney. Her attorney then cashed the check and collected his legal fees and returned the balance to Mrs. Van Divner who then used the remaining proceeds to pay Mrs. Druyvesteyn's living expenses and insurance expenses.

-Roy Gean, Jr.

Attached was a verification that Linda Van Divner signed attesting to the accuracy of said document.

Well, that was about as worthless a bunch of BS as I had seen in a long time. I guess Troy was equally impressed as he immediately sent a letter to Judge Cox.

**May 13, 2011**

Honorable James O. Cox
Sebastian County Circuit Judge

Dear Judge Cox:

Please set this above referenced matter for a one hour in Aid of Judgment hearing. I'm requesting that you set this hearing and that you order Linda Van Divner to appear. Specifically, I have finally just received responses to my Post Judgment Interrogatories that I propounded back in February even though you ordered them due to me by April 25. These responses are inadequate. For instance, I have asked for banks or institutions where any of this money was deposited and they said it was cashed and spent on "living expenses." Do they expect me to believe that this money was held in cash and that they walked around passing out $100 bills to pay her living expenses?

Further, I do not have any way to know whether these living expenses that they describe in paragraph 3 were expended using funds from this settlement or from the other bond that Ms. Druyvesteyn received separate from this bond. Nothing they have given me helps whatsoever to trace these funds.

The other problem is that the Circuit Clerk wrote a check to Mr. Gean's clients for the balance of the judgment. You issued a judgment to my client following appeal for $200,000. But I believe deposit may have been higher than that amount. I have asked the Clerk and Mr. Gean to provide me with a copy of the check to get the exact amount that was issued out of the account. They both say they do not have a copy of the check or any record of the amount. I would like for you to consider ordering the Clerk to search for records of the check written in the month that the Order to pay funds was entered.

-Troy Gaston

### JAMES O. COX
Circuit Judge, Division VI

May 19, 2011
RE: Terry Druyvestein, v Lois Druyvesteyn et al.

Dear Counselors:

This letter will confirm that the above styled case has been set for a one hour hearing to begin at 9:30 a.m. on Wednesday, June 8, 2011 in room 203 of the Sebastian County Courts Building, Ft. Smith.

-Kim Dodson, Trial Ct. Asst.

As with all of the dates set for action, they come and go and nothing happens. So on July 15, 2011, my attorney Troy prepared a Motion for Contempt.

### MOTION FOR CONTEMPT

Comes now the plaintiff, Terry Druyvestein, by and through his attorney Troy Gaston, and for his Motion for Contempt does state and allege as follows:

1. This Court directed Linda Van Divner to provide responses to the Plaintiff's previously propounded Interrogatories within twenty days of the Court's entry of a Judgment. The Judgment was entered on June 13, 2011. It is now July 14, 2011. More than 20 days have expired and Linda Van Divner should be held in contempt of court. Linda Van Divner should be ordered to pay all attorney fees and cost associated with this Motion and the previous hearing which hearing was held largely due to her failure to provide "believable" responses.

2. The Plaintiff prays for an Order of this Court holding Linda Van Divner in contempt for failure to provide timely responses pursuant to this Court's Order of June 13, 2011. And for the Contempt Order to hold her liable for $600 in attorney fees associated with the previous hearing and this Motion.

Wherefore the Plaintiff prays for an Order of this Court holding Linda Van Divner in contempt of court and for her to pay attorney fees and cost and for all other relief to which Plaintiff is entitled to.

-Troy Gaston


No motion of Contempt was granted.

It is hard to understand that Judge Cox does not respond to any sense of urgency in this matter. I personally am of the opinion that he holds a grudge against us for appealing this case in the first place and embarrassing him because of the rather severe thrashing he took from the Appeals Court. If it had not been for his errors in his initial ruling, we would not be in this predicament now. So now, he does not grant our motion for Contempt and also sets a new hearing date. Perhaps he is on vacation, I don't know.

JAMES O. COX
Circuit Judge, Division VI

Aug. 30, 2011
RE: Terry Druyvestein, v Lois Druyvesteyn, et al.

Dear Counselors:

This letter will advise that the above styled case has been set for a 1 hour hearing to begin at 10:00 A.M. on Friday, Sept. 30, 2011 in room 203 of the Sebastian County Courts Building.

-Kim Dodson, Ct. Manager

I see Kim Dodson has gone from the Trial Ct. Asst. to now the Ct. Manager. Good for Kim. Careers come and go and our case just outlasts them all. I wish the judge would retire.

Perhaps I am growing a little "flippant" with this whole case. I have to cool it as it is pissing me off too much. One thing I have learned in my almost 80 years of life is "don't take things personally" and don't get upset when things don't go your way. Of course that is easy to say but sometimes hard to put into practice. I will make a bigger effort to hold my emotions in check. When you let your emotions run your body, your brain has kicked out of gear. You then suffer the consequences, don't you think? Come on, I need some support here!

One day after the Judge sets the hearing date, Linda writes a letter to Judge Cox.

Aug. 31, 2011
Honorable Judge Cox
RE: Terry Druyvestein v Summit Brokerage et al.

Dear Honorable Cox:

Enclosed is a copy of the Amended Answers to Interrogatories that were found to be "unbelievable." As you will see, the answers have not changed, the wording is more elaborate and I have provided documentary evidence to confirm the answers. Also enclosed is the completed Schedule of Property. I have forwarded the same to Roy Gean Jr., and ask that he will file them with the court once he has signed them.

133

I am in receipt of the transcripts of the June 8, 2011 hearing. As you will see by the copies of the enclosed checks, the original $208,830.72 check from Summit Brokerage was made payable to Lois Druyvesteyn but sent to Roy Gean Jr. of Gean, Gean & Gean. As stated in my original answers, Mr. Roy Gean Jr. drove all the way to Kansas to have Lois Druyvesteyn endorse the check. Then you will see by the stamp on the back of the check that it was deposited in an account in Ft. Smith, Arkansas. Then Roy Gean Jr. wrote me, Linda Van Divner, a check for $105,625.72. Although the check was not also endorsed by Roy Gean Jr., the check clearly shows what account it was deposited into which appears to be from the same account that Gean, Gean & Gean Law firm wrote the check to me. I never really understood why the check was made payable to me instead of my mother, especially since he had mother sign the original check. It did not matter though, because I knew it was her money and that is why I have used it on her care. I asked Roy Gean for a statement of services which I assumed would explain why he retained the $103,205 but have not received any such statement to date.

In the hearing, it appears that I am being referred to as uncooperative. I hired an attorney in Kansas to help me help my mother complete these answers. Roy Gean kept sending him unsigned, unfile-stamped documents which were not sufficient for the lawyer to be comfortable in advising what to do. The lawyer's paralegal had to obtain the information directly from the courts.

I am not uncooperative and am only trying to be a good steward to my mother to the best of my ability. Please send me copies of any future pleadings so I do not get blindsided about hearings and other court procedures after the fact.

I am facing this cover letter and the first few pages of the attachments to the interrogatories. I am mailing the full package via regular mail to Roy Gean and to your chambers. Please also let me know if the court needs anything further to finalize this matter on behalf of my mother.

In closing, I would like to thank you for your ruling. We all know that Mr. Druyvesteyn changed the beneficiary because of the horrible way his family treated my mother at the family picnic. I was baffled when I learned the Court of Appeals had overturned your ruling on hearsay vs. written documentation.

-Linda Van Divner
For Lois Druyvesteyn

Well, I don't know if she was wanting to rack up some points with the judge by backing him up against the appeals court but it probably did not hurt. The Judge in my view could use a little backing as he sure had screwed this case up. What really got to me though, was her comment that Humpy had changed the TOD because of the horrible way in which the family treated Lois at the reunion. Wow! Lois was the one who did not want my sisters to visit with Humpy and went out of her way to keep them from visiting him. She is also the one who had Humpy buried in her cemetery plot against his direct instructions to the contrary. But I digress. That was a long time ago in this book and the facts speak for themselves. Lois was a gold digger, plain and simple, and it appears she trained her daughter to be the same. The fact that Roy Gean Jr. made the check for $105,625.72 payable to Linda Van Divner and not to Lois speaks volumes to me as to who is in charge.

On Sept. 7, 2011, Troy wrote a letter to Roy Gean.
Dear Roy,

I am in receipt of Linda Van Divner's Responses to Interrogatories. Of course, I provided those responses to my client Terry Druyvestein since he has been very upset about the length of time it has taken to get these responses.

Mr. Druyvestein is taking the position that he believes that your firm should pay him the amount of $103,205 due to the fact that this money never should have been paid out from Summit Brokerage Services to Lois but instead should have been paid directly to him. I have always enjoyed a good relationship with your firm and would hope that I would not have to request any payment of services from you. However, my client has made it absolutely clear that he is going to pursue these funds whether it is through me or another counsel. I am providing you with this letter to give you an opportunity to provide me with any legal authority which you contend allows you to keep the money that should have been paid to Terry Druyvestein. If you do not provide the funds within the next ten days, then we will have no choice but to proceed with asking the Court to order that the funds be paid over to the Druyvestein family. Also, I appreciate your kind cooperation.

-Troy

I think it is a very difficult thing for an attorney to sue another. They have, after all, the same fraternity they belong to – the same professional organization and in many cases the same country club or exercise clubs which they attend. So the wording has to be guarded. I saw this in the letter where Troy is careful with his wording that we are "requesting" payment of services from his firm. I would have liked to have said "It's pay up time, slime ball." There is no doubt in my mind that Roy was a major contributor to this scam. He knew that Lois had no idea that she could lay claim to the bond monies and as a consequence he took the horrendous fee of $103,205. He drove to Kansas, had Lois sign over the check from Summit Brokerage in the amount of $208,830 and then issued a check back to Linda, not Lois, in the amount of $105,625. Now, this transaction is very suspicious all around. I had always wanted Lois to testify at trial or at least be deposed and see how it was possible for her to get around the conversations Humpy had with me and Loretta, all of this with her present, and with these conversations directly addressing the TOD for the bond fund to be received by my family. I do not think Lois could lie about that. Linda, however, would not have any problems with that and that is why I never got to deal with Lois. Linda had controlled Lois's entire financial and medical life through through these past years of our lawsuit. It dawned on me that this was truly a case of "undue influence" as Linda had taken possession of all of Lois's property. Her duplexes, her checking accounts, savings accounts, everything. It would appear that Lois was a good teacher. She taught her daughter really well.

I started this chapter with the news that Sue Rose has passed away. I will end it with the news that her husband Bob Rose has also passed away, one year to the month after Sue. It now leaves their son Jon and his wife Shanna with the two grandchildren Irene and Alex as the sole survivors of the main family in Humpy's life. I mention them as the sole survivors as I do not count Lois as family. I wonder how old "Hub" is surviving. He also was a true friend for Humpy.

*The Rose Family*
*top; Shanna, Alex, Bob - bottom; Irene, Humpy, Sue*

# CHAPTER TEN

## Attorneys are Divided

Troy had asked Judge Cox to set a hearing to force Linda and Roy to answer questions concerning their distribution of the bond funds. Linda had now finally responded to some degree. Roy Gean Jr. had not responded about his role in taking $103,205 from the total.

Roy Gean Jr. has now decided that he wants out of the lawsuit. His client Linda no longer cooperates and apparently does not want to be represented by Roy and it appears that a split is eminent. He really has taken the posture that he should be let out of the lawsuit. Roy asks Judge Cox for ten days so he can "study the law and write a brief on whether the money he is holding has to be paid back into the court treasury."

Well, I am certain of two things. First, that ten days does not really mean ten. Second, that it appears that Roy will not willingly pay the money back to the court and will drag this out for as long of a time as is possible. Lawyers have almost unlimited means to drag things out and make things as expensive as possible for anyone who might dare to "sue" them. The nerve of it all.

I have concerns and send an email to Troy on Oct. 3, 2011. Troy:

1. Concerning what the situation is with Linda. She received the money and now she appears to be "out of the loop" when it comes to paying it back. She received Lois's duplexes in Barling and claims those were needed to take care of Lois's living expenses. This was done at the same time I should have received the bond money from the account Humpy wanted my family to have. Why can't we foreclose on them? Won't Judge Cox allow us to do this? Also will Judge Cox allow us to be reimbursed for legal expenses and lost interest to pursue this action? Interest from the time they wrongfully received the money and legal expenses from the time we won the appeal?

2. Concerning Roy Gean's "fee" of $103,205, why is Linda not the one responsible to sue Roy for the return of it? It was her or her mother, I'm not certain who, that in reality paid Roy the money. For what and under what agreement we do not know. The check from the court was given to Lois, she signed the check over to Roy Gean Jr. and he sends a check to Linda – not to Lois! So who is responsible?

3. Right now I don't know where we stand. You have been very busy, I know, but it now seems we are at a hold-off. Their side will not respond, the judge does not make them, and we are stymied. I wish I was closer to attend to this better.

I have to leave for South Dakota on Wednesday as my mother is not doing well. I will be gone about a week. You can reach me at my brother's place. Hope to hear from you before I leave.

Troy returns my email on Oct. 4, 2011.

Terry:

I am suing for interest, legal fees and the apartments. Roy's 10 days, as usual, are up and we have not heard from him. I will file the complaint tomorrow. I am serving Linda with papers personally and not going through Roy since the two of them seem to have parted ways. We are at a standstill due to Roy getting the 10-day extension from Judge Cox. But the time is up and we are suing both of them.

I do not hear anything by Nov. 13 so I email Troy.

Troy:

On the 5th you were going to file our complaint against Linda and Roy Gean Jr. I would like to know the actual date the judge is to hear the complaint and what kind of time schedule you anticipate on this case going forward. Could you give me an idea as to what to expect and what, if anything, I need to do at this end? Also, what happens to the case we won against Lois and how does this all fit together? Do we now have to proceed on two fronts

Troy responds on Nov. 14, 2011.

Terry:

Right now our only problem is serving Linda. I have a process server looking to serve her. Since this is technically a "new lawsuit" against Linda asking for new relief, we have to serve her with the papers. We still have a judgment against Lois and her estate, but I do anticipate that we will eventually get the money from Roy and Linda. I have talked to the judge and he is ready to have a hearing as soon as I serve her. I have copied my assistant on this asking her to give me a status report on serving Linda.

Troy's assistant Dena continues the next day: I have spoken with the server this morning and they told me that Linda was served on November 10th (5 days ago) I have also been calling for the past week to check if a probate estate had been opened for Lois. As of today nothing has been opened. I checked with Troy and he says that is probably "because Lois no longer has any property to probate."

We have now just learned that Lois had passed away several weeks ago. There evidently is no requirement for anyone, including Linda who has been speaking for Lois, to tell you that the person you are suing has passed away. It is only by chance that one learns these things. I still do not know the exact date nor even the cause of Lois's death. In a way, I was saddened by Lois's passing. She never had been antagonistic to me directly and I greatly regret that she never was allowed by her daughter nor her attorney to testify in our original lawsuit. I also cannot help but think that her last years were not quality time and perhaps she gave Humpy some good days, at least in the initial year or two. I guess it is best to look at the best side of people.

On Nov. 14, Roy filed his Answers to the Complaint which we had filed against him.

Comes the third defendant, Roy Gean Jr., and for his answer to the Complaint for Creation of a Constructive Trust, for Judgment against Linda Van Divner, and for relief pursuant to the Fraudulent Transfer Act, alleges and States:

1. That 3rd Defendant, Roy Gean Jr. is not a proper party in this litigation.

2. That Plaintiff has no legal claim against 3rd Defendant, Roy Gean Jr.

3. That Plaintiff has failed to state facts for which relief may be granted.

4. That there is lack of privity of contract or a relationship allowing such claim.

5. That moneys paid by defendant Lois Druyvesteyn to Roy Gean Jr. were earned monies which could be expected for his services.

6. That the contract for services between Lois Druyvesteyn and Roy Gean was a typical contract between attorneys and clients for which clients pay attorney's fees.

7. There is no connection or basis for Plaintiff to Claim against Roy Gean Jr.

8. That Plaintiff made up his own mind to pay Lois. (through his failure to post a bond with the court to hold the funds while appeal was made) and as such the monies paid to Roy Gean Jr. are his to keep.

9. That Plaintiff paid money to Lois to avoid other matters that the law required of him in connection with an appeal.

10. That Roy Gean Jr. denies he ever received any monies which belonged to plaintiff.

WHEREFORE; the defendant Roy Gean Jr. prays that the Complaint for Creation of a Constructive Trust against him be denied, and that he be awarded his fees and costs herein expended, and further, that said defendant prays for proper relief.

Well, Roy certainly looks at it differently than I do and to top it off he is asking the judge to award him legal fees expended and it looks like all other damages, whatever they are. I surmise from the first part of his "Answers to our Complaint" that Roy wishes to show that there is no legal basis that we can use to connect him to our case. There is no contract; there is no communication nor anything making him liable to me. He simply was paid by Lois for legal work which he had done for her and the money which Lois paid him with was as far as he knew, Lois's money to spend as she pleased. The second part says that it was my fault that the money was not protected and that the monies would not have been dispersed had I provided the proper bonding to hold it with the Court. So essentially it is not adequate to file an appeal and if the money is spent before the appeal is heard, then too bad for me. Don't expect to get it back. This is a perfect example of what I dislike about the legal profession. What is clearly right has nothing to do with Roy's actions. It was legal to take the money, spend it quick, so forget who the court eventually says should be the recipient of the money. Too bad, it's spent, it's gone, get along another way, we owe you nothing. I will see what Troy has to say about this. It occurs to me to ask Troy, again, why it is not Linda who should be responsible to sue Roy to return the money Lois gave him? He did not win the case and Roy's fee is so extravagant that it must be a contingency fee based on his actual winning of the case. Is not getting your verdict overturned actually "losing the case?" Should not the contingency fee (which means contingent upon winning) be given back if you actually lose the case on appeal? Why did they allow Roy such a huge fee anyway? Was it because they both looked at it as an illicit gain and if they got something out of it good, if not, well nothing lost? Lois, for certain knew that the money was not to go to her. Linda perhaps felt differently and Roy was all too happy to take half of it. It is now official that Roy is off the case for Linda.

On Nov. 28, Judge Cox received a letter from Paige Young, an attorney in Springdale, Arkansas, that designated her as Linda's council.

She informed us that legally, Linda had 30 days or until Dec. 4th to respond to the complaint which was served against her. She also requested additional time to familiarize herself with the case and was not sure yet if any discovery would be necessary before any hearing. A copy was also sent to Roy.

The judge granted additional time for her to familiarize and take any discovery. "Please advise the Court when discovery has been completed and this case will be placed on the docket at that time."

On Dec. 12, 2011, Judge Cox issued the notice that a two-hour Pre Trial hearing was set on his docket for 9:30 AM on Jan. 13, 2012. How time continues to go by.

On Dec. 18, 2011, I email Troy with some questions.
Troy:

1. Is it best for me to attend the pretrial hearing or the trial itself? I understand by reading between the lines, a lot will be decided at the pretrial hearing and maybe the actual trial will simply be the judge's decision and it may turn out to be shorter than the hearing? In any case, I am doubtful that I can afford to come to both so what is your advice as to which one is most important for me to attend?

2. What preparations should I make for the hearing or trial? The original case has already been tried and we were awarded the bond Humpy wanted my family to have. Everything since that trial has been maneuvering on the part of Linda and Roy in their attempt not to give

any of the money back. Linda has been especially adept at transferring monies out of Lois's name and into her own accounts to the point where Lois had no monies at the time of her death. I understand that you are preparing to cite a lot of law as to how this was not legal on their part to do. I think we need to contest the way in which Roy drove to Kansas, had Lois sign over the check, then took it and deposit it in his account from which he gave Linda, not Lois, a check for about half of the money back. Who was in charge here? It certainly was not Lois.

3. The only testimony I can actually provide is what happened between Lois and our family and all of that was given at the original trial which we prevailed in, on appeal. What else can I offer the judge in these new cases? I can review my original testimonies and be prepared for anything with respect to the original case. It seems that 90% or more will be up to you citing the "Fraudulent Transfer Act" and other related case law which you are now preparing. So perhaps my presence would primarily be for the judge's benefit as it may be harder to rule against me if I am actually present. If I come to the pre-trial hearing, I will plan to arrive in Ft. Smith on Thursday afternoon so we can discuss things before the hearing set for 9:30 AM on Friday.

The next day, Dec. 19, 2011, Troy emailed me back.
Terry:

If you can only come to one, the hearing or the trial, I would recommend that you come to the actual trial. The pre-trial will not include any testimony. It will be attorneys arguing, but at the trial there will be testimony from witnesses and I might need you to be one of those witnesses. The thing I might need you to testify about is to establish that Lois and Linda knew about the potential for litigation before they transferred the duplexes into Linda's name. This is a fact we might have to prove.

I immediately responded to Troy:
What you say is interesting. As you recall, right after the death of Humpy, Jon Rose filed a suit against Lois which you handled. Was

anything involved there which would have made Lois nervous and prompted her to transfer property as quickly as possible to Linda? I personally do not know the actual date of the transfer of the duplexes from Humpy's and Lois's names to Linda. I think you should get the actual date as soon as you can. I think Lois, or perhaps it was Linda, realized that there was reason for them to worry about claims against Lois' properties and quickly transferred ownership of all they could to lower that risk.

Troy responded:

By saying that he had already obtained the actual date of the transfer of the duplexes and that those records show that it was soon after Lois received the notice from Summit naming Lois as the beneficiary of the account held by my family. The point being that Linda and Lois, when transferring the duplex titles to Linda, already would have known that the ownership of the account was being held up and challenged in court. Troy repeated that it really would not be the best use of my time to come to the pre-trial hearing. He would ask Jon Rose to come and sit by him for the "family."

**Jan. 4, 2012**, I email Troy.

Troy:

I realize that some of what I am writing is a duplication of what I have sent to you previously so will try to avoid that. I addressed one thing that Linda wrote in her letter to Judge Cox about how her mother was mistreated by my family at the last reunion. This is complete BS and if it comes up in court I would love to address a response. It was Lois who shut Humpy's family out by not letting my two sisters visit Humpy. It had been Lois who would not let Humpy be alone with any of the family members at the reunion. It was Lois who cut Humpy off from all of his past friends and finally family. It was Lois who completely ignored Humpy's and all of our family's wishes after his death. No one was invited to come to the funeral, Humpy was not buried in the spot reserved for him next to his previous wife Bobbie, but instead was buried in Lois's cemetery where she now lies between Humpy and her previous husband. Lois did not honor Humpy's wishes with respect to passing along family heirlooms which were designated as going to my family. Lois tried to take personal property from the Rose family which did not belong to her. You should be familiar with that case as you handled it for Jon Rose. Lois cut all of the Druyvestein family off from seeing or associating with Humpy; that was a disgrace, not the other way around that Lois was mistreated by Humpy's blood family.

I would also like to emphasize that after Linda took control with Roy's help, she did the same thing. We never were able to get Lois to testify, never were able to talk to her to explain anything; she never appeared in court, never took a deposition. Judge Cox allowed this to go on from when we filed our first case in September of 2007 to October of 2011. That is four years they were able to stall and Lois was never even deposed, let alone being forced to testify under oath. She was put "under wraps" so to speak.

I talked to Jon Rose and he said that he would be glad to "sit in" for me at the pre-trial if he was able to schedule it in. He said he would get back to me, but he has not done so, as of this date. Perhaps you can contact him with more details and remind him of the date. I will continue to plan to come to the trial, assuming the judge grants us one. Let me know when a date is set.

Troy emailed me on Jan. 10, 2012.

Terry:

Jon called and he cannot be in court on the day of our pre-trial hearing. I have been in negotiation with Ms. Young and she has agreed to accept service of a new lawsuit against Linda (which will say the same thing as the old one) which will take care of her motion to dismiss on the grounds that the old lawsuit does not apply to her. In exchange, I agreed to do Linda's deposition by phone.

I thought that there would be no depositions before the pre-trial hearing. I asked Troy if they would also depose me. He said that he did not think so. He said that the burden of proof was on us now so he was deposing Linda to demonstrate how she and Lois transferred properties from her mother's name to protect them from the pending litigation.

# CHAPTER ELEVEN
## A New Ballgame

A Complaint naming Lois Druyvesteyn as First Defendant, Linda Van Divner as Second Defendant, and Roy Gean Jr. now as Third Defendant is filed with the Sebastian County Circuit Court in Ft. Smith, Arkansas and defendants are served.

What a course of events. After five years of legal filings, court cases, appeals and even a Supreme Court case, we are at square one. We won the initial legal battle against Lois and her estate presumably, but we have nothing to show for it except having paid a lot of legal bills and created a huge amount of work for legal assistants, court reporters, judges, etc. etc. This was all done because a lawyer did not do what he knew was just, but rather he pursued a path he felt could be deemed as legal. Lois clearly knew what Humpy wanted when he made me and my family the TOD on the Ford Motor Company bond and how, in the name of justice, could her attorney keep her from testifying or giving a deposition to hide this fact for five years? How can a judge and legal system allow this to occur? There is little doubt in my mind that between the two sides in the legal battle and the court system, the hours spent by witnesses, lawyers, paralegals, court reporters, court judges and staff, that more money has already been spent than what was at stake. Any sane person must recognize that one really needs to ask the question

– who created this problem? Who should be paying these costs when all of the facts finally come out? If courts would not be so reluctant to award prevailing parties a reimbursement of their legal expenses, the lawyers would be much less inclined to take up a case which is clearly not justified. I put this problem squarely on Judge Cox in this case. Will he award us reimbursement of legal expenses? How could he allow Lois's attorney Roy Gean Jr. to walk around the system with delays and even miss filing deadlines? It also seems that he has taken offense at our reluctance to accept his rulings and when he is remanded to redo his ruling on appeal, he does it in stern words, but words which seem to be empty and which are not enforced.

On **Feb. 12, 2012**, I have a conference call with my attorney.

I am confused by the case and Troy has to get me back in line. My problem is that I keep going back to what happened in the original case, the case which we won and obtained a judgment against Lois. Our case now is separate and independent of the first case. It is now a case against Linda to get money back which she obtained from Lois and was used to take care of her mother's living expenses and was now being used by Linda as sort of an inheritance. The burden of proof is now on us to show that Linda abused her position and used funds, which she should not have been using, because she was aware of the fact that these funds were part of the lawsuit we had against her mother. Troy says this is not as easy as it sounds – that Linda will attempt to show that she needed these funds for the upkeep of her mother and was justified in using them as her mother had no other funds left. OK, so Linda had all of her mother's assets transferred to her name, including two duplexes without debt, her own bond given to her by Humpy, a life insurance policy for how much I don't know, Humpy's checking account and receipts from much personal property which I can't say that I know much about. The bottom line is that Lois then needed the funds from our bond because she had already given all of her other assets to her daughter, even the new house she bought in Kansas. In addition, Linda – not Lois – was the recipient of the check from Roy Gean Jr., giving her their share of the $208,830 check from the court. Linda had testified at the original trial that they had to work to "spend down" her mother's assets to make her mother eligible for public assistance with respect to assisted living expenses. Spending down apparently meant transferring ownerships to Linda. This "spending down" was being done during the time of our lawsuit against Lois. Is that not proof that funds were not only being hidden from the government but also from my family?

Troy says that interrogatories from second defendant, Roy Gean Jr. are due by March 7, 2012. He sends me a list of the interrogatory questions and suggested information which we will testify to. These include the regular boiler plate with names, addresses and how we will testify. This is our combined response.

1) Terry Druyvestein will testify that the Druyvestein family was nothing but cordial to Lois Druyvesteyn up to and until the time that Lois took a stepped-up and more aggressive roll to drive all other friends and family away from Humpy. This odd and aggressive behavior started to become apparent during and after a visit that was made by the Druyvesteins in 2006. This behavior was magnified in the way Lois prevented any family from visiting or even finding out the medical condition of Humpy when he was hospitalized in the winter of 2006/2007. This behavior was manifest in the way Lois handled the final wishes of Humpy in preparing and conducting his funeral services and carrying out his final wishes which were related to Terry and his wife Loretta in their 2006 visit.

2) Terry Druyvestein will also testify that it was Linda Van Diviner, the daughter of Lois Druyvesteyn, who took all messages, was to relay said messages to Lois, and who was the person responsible for handling all correspondence and dealings with Lois from the time of the initial discovery of a mistake having been made in the original TOD forms, through all correspondence in trying to resolve and correct the error that was made, throughout the course of the initial lawsuit meant to rectify the error and throughout all the legal actions since that time.

3) Loretta Druyvestein will testify as to all of the parts of the testimony above that she was a party to and in addition to a telephone conversation that she had with Linda Van Divner in which Linda indicated that she and Lois were interested in resolving the "error" in TOD documents and that they did not wish to "claim" the bond money which was to go to the Druyvestein family.

4) Jon Rose will testify as to the selfish and mean attitude and actions which Lois exhibited when she began a program of driving a wedge between his Grandfather Humpy and his family and Humpy's old friends in their neighborhood. He will testify as to how Lois prevented his family from seeing Humpy in the hospital and how Lois went against Humpy's burial plans and how they were not even allowed to attend the funeral services. He will also testify to her actions immediately following the funeral.

In addition, it was stated that Terry Druyvestein has personal notes and phone conversation records that he will make reference to. (I am thankful that I did make regular notes of conversations in a diary type notebook with my files.)

On **Jan. 6** we receive a "Motion to Quash Deposition" from Paige Young, Linda's attorney. (On all of these lawsuits it appears that the first response is not to cooperate but rather attempt to get out of the lawsuit all together.)

Reasons for this motion are that: Ms. Van Divner has filed a Motion to dismiss based on the premise that there is not a properly filed claim in a court having jurisdiction, that the deposition is attempting to require action on an out-of-state, non-party to the alleged cause of action, the court lacks personal jurisdiction over Ms. Van Divner, the notice of deposition is insufficient to require her appearance and if none of this works, requests that the deposition be conducted over the phone. In addition, third defendant Roy Gean files a motion to dismiss.

On **Feb. 6** an order to dismiss is signed by Judge Cox as the dismissal is agreed to by both parties.

Apparently there are some legal snafus and Troy has to redo the complaint. A new complaint is filed naming Linda Van Diviner as First Defendant and Roy Gean as Second Defendant. Lois is dead after all and why she was shown on the original complaint I do not know and don't even ask. Just another couple months lost. So the new complaint now is: AMENDED COMPLAINT FOR CREATION OF A CONSTRUCTIVE TRUST, FOR JUDGMENT AGAINST LINDA VAN DIVNER AND FOR RELIEF PURSUANT TO ARKANSAS STATUTE 4-59-204, ET. SEQ.

**The Facts Common to all Causes** of action were as follows:

1. T. Druyvestein was named as a pay-on-death beneficiary for an account held in the name of Humpy Druyvesteyn. T. Druyvestein communicated with Lois Druyvesteyn, and her daughter, Linda Van Divner, and also with Lois's financial planner Donna Young. T. Druyvestein was named as a TOD (transfer-on-death) beneficiary for an account held in these conversations and all three parties were made aware that T. Druyvestein would make a claim to the funds which had previously been titled in the name of Humpy Druyvesteyn. However, an error had occurred. The financial planner testified in CV-2007-1383 that she made a clerical error and Lois was mistakenly listed as TOD beneficiary for the subject account despite Humpy's intentions. The trial court in CV-2007-1383 ruled that the written document controlled and that Lois was the proper payee. The Arkansas Court of Appeals has ruled that Plaintiff is entitled to the funds based upon a constructive trust. The trial court then granted a judgment in favor of T. Druyvestein in CV-2007-1383 for the full amount of $208,830. Van Divner continued to act on her mother's behalf and responded to post-judgment interrogatories. The amount and the location of said funds were kept from the Defendant and his counsel due to interrogatory responses being, in the trial court's words, "inadequate and unbelievable." Plaintiff only learned of the location and amount of funds on August 31, 2011 through interrogatory responses filed by Ms. Linda Van Divner after a Motion for Contempt was filed.

2. Van Divner admitted in her cover letter to the court that she deposited all funds from CV-2007-1383 into her own checking account except for that portion withheld by Mr. Gean for his fees and expenses in litigating CV-2007-1383. Van Divner's letter can be fairly read as demonstrating that she did not pay consideration for the funds. Also, even if she did pay Lois' medical expenses with the funds she did so without any legal duty and protected her own assets by preventing the Medicaid look back provision from disturbing previous transfers of assets to Van Divner.

3. Van Divner alleged in her letter that Mr. Gean collected $103,205 in fees for his work in CV-2007-1383 but has refused to provide her with an accounting of such fees.

4. Mr. Roy Gean and Ms. Linda Van Divner took control of the entire funds to which the Plaintiff is entitled, $208,830.72. The funds were divided with Mr. Gean taking $103,205 and Ms. Divner took $105,625.72.

**Claim for a Constructive Trust Against Both Defendants**

1. A constructive trust should be created over the funds held by both Mr. Gean and Ms. Van Divner and judgment entered against them in favor of Mr. Terry Druyvestein. The judgment against Ms. Van Divner should be for the full amount of $208,830.72 since she has concealed the location of said funds for more than one year and defrauded the court with her previous interrogatory responses which failed to reveal that the funds were placed into an account with her name on it. These transfers were made as a result, at very least, of a mistake. Van Divner had an affirmative duty to reveal the location of the funds to the court in as much as she had appeared before the court and requested relief and was aware that the court had entered a judgment over said funds. Any time that funds have been wrongly transferred to a third party, whether or not there is fraud involved, this court has a duty to create a constructive trust over those funds and order them transferred to the proper recipient. Additional grounds for a constructive trust include the fact that Mr. Gean and Ms. Van Divner made the transfer without the

written knowledge or consent of Lois and without consulting any court or guardian acting on Lois' behalf.

### Claim for relief under Arkansas Statute 4-59-204 et. al.

1. Lois Druyvesteyn's estate is insolvent under the definition of Ark. Stat. Ann. 4-59-202. This was known or reasonably should have been known to both Defendants by virtue of their relationship with Lois as her legal counsel and daughter.

2. Van Divner and Mr. Gean were both aware of T. Druyvestein's claim at the time that they made transfers to themselves using Lois' own funds.

3. Post-judgment discovery responses and subpoenas revealed Lois did not have sufficient funds to satisfy the judgment upon her death. The above mentioned transfers by Lois have left her estate unable to pay her proper creditor, T. Druyvestein.

4. The transfer to Linda Van Divner was not made for value received and therefore must be voided pursuant to Ark. Statute. "When a debtor makes a transfer, aware of a creditors claim, and does not receive value, then the transfer is considered fraudulent and may be undone." The Statute recognizes the trial courts "equitable powers" to avoid injustice.

5. Any funds owed to Roy Gean are the debt of Lois. They should not be paid with T. Druyvestein's money. Linda Van Divner alleges in her letter, Exhibit A, that Mr. Gean's fees charged for that transfer is not based upon value. In fact, Mr. Gean's fees are many times more than what opposing counsel billed for similar work on the same matter. That transaction should also be voided and the funds transferred back to Mr. Druyvestein.

6. Finally, Linda Van Divner caused a transfer of real estate to be made without consideration of the debt Lois owed to Mr. Druyvestein. This property consists of two duplex properties in Ft. Smith which Humpy had deeded to Lois. (legal descriptions attached) These properties were transferred without consideration for the debt potentially owed to Mr. Druyvestein. This transaction should therefore

be set aside if the Judgment is not satisfied by the payment of funds by the two defendants.

Wherefore the Plaintiff prays for an Order of this Court granting the relief set-out herein and for all other relief to which they may be entitled.

A certification of Service was given on the 8th of February 2012 to:
1. 1 Paige E. Young, Attorney for First Defendant Linda Van Divner.
2. 2 Roy Gean Jr., the second defendant.
3. 3 Honorable James Cox, Sebastian County Circuit Judge.
4.

On **Feb. 15**, Roy Gean, Jr. responded with his answers to the AMENDED COMPLAINT FOR CREATION OF A CONSTRUCTIVE TRUST, FOR JUDGMENT AGAINST LINDA VAN DIVNER AND FOR RELIEF PURSUANT TO ARKANSAS STATUTE 4-59-204, ET. SEQ.

1. The second defendant, Roy Gean, Jr., is not a proper party to this litigation.

2. That plaintiff, Druyvestein, has no legal claim or standing against this responding second defendant and additionally plaintiff has no direct relationship with said second defendant.

3. That plaintiff, Druyvestein, has failed to state facts upon which relief can be granted against second defendant, Gean.

4. That there is lack of privity of contract or relationship as to any such claim as set forth by the plaintiff against second defendant, Gean.

5. That any sums of money paid by Lois Druyvesteyn to said second defendant, Gean, were earned by said second defendant and for which said defendant could expect payment. That there was no contract or any agreement or any basis for any litigation by said plaintiff against said second defendant, Roy Gean, Jr. That the plaintiff has no standing

to question the fee arrangement of this said second defendant with his client.

6. That the Contract between Lois Druyvesteyn and second defendant, Gean, was a typical contract between attorneys and clients for clients to pay attorneys their fees and other arrangements for cost and expenses.

7. That there was not any connection or basis for the plaintiff to make a claim against this defendant, Gean.

8. That plaintiff made up his own mind to pay Lois Druyvesteyn the sum of money which he paid to her (by failing to post a supersedeas bond) and in connection therewith, the defendant, Roy Gean, was not involved.

9. That plaintiff paid money to Lois Druyvesteyn to avoid other matters that the law required of him in connection with an appeal he filed against Summit Brokerage Services, Inc., and against Lois Druyvesteyn which was filed in the case of Druyvestein V. Summit and Lois Druyvesteyn, Case No. CV-2007-1383.

10. That this defendant denies that he ever received any monies that belonged to the plaintiff, Druyvestein, or to which the plaintiff may assert an interest. That Druyvestein apparently is claiming that money was his, even though he is the one who made the arrangement and directed the payment by the Summit Brokerage and for the same to be paid to said Lois Druyvesteyn. (This again by his failure to post a supersedeas bond)

11. That as additional affirmative defenses, the defendant asserts failure to name necessary party, lack of fraud, lack of fraudulent intent, estoppel, release, statute of limitations and waiver.

12. That it is admitted that Roy Gean Jr., is an attorney licensed to practice law in the State of Arkansas and is a resident of the State of Arkansas.

13. That it is admitted that the Trial Court ruled in favor of the Client of the second defendant.

14. That, unless specifically admitted herein, all allegations set forth in the aforesaid Amended Complaint are denied.

WHEREFORE, premises considered, the second defendant prays that the Amended Complaint be denied and dismissed and further prays for all other relief to which this second defendant is entitled including reimbursement of attorney's fees and costs herein incurred by the second defendant.

Well it appears that Mr. Gean is indignant that he is being called into this case. When he clearly has no substantive argument and is clearly in the wrong, he takes the offensive and acts indignant and really tries to intimidate anyone who thinks he is not in the right. He even has the balls to ask for reimbursement of his attorney's fees. In reality, he took half of an illicit gain, blames me for allowing the money to be distributed to his client and then to him, all this because my attorney did not post bond to keep the funds held while on appeal. He admits only that the trial court ruled in his favor and because he got his money before the appeals court overturned the trial court, he should be able to keep it because he "gave" it to Lois and she paid him his fee.

He is partially right in one thing. My attorney should have asked me if I wanted to post the bond and hold the money in the court. I never knew of this requirement to post a supersedeas bond. I thought since the decision of the trial court was on appeal, that the money would automatically be held. In any event, my attorney should have asked me about this. I think my attorney either did not know or was too busy to consider the option so did not ask me. Had he done so I would most certainly have at least considered posting the bond. As it turns out we certainly would have saved a lot of time and money if we had.

On **Feb. 22, 2012**, the second defendant Roy Gean Jr. responds to CV-2012-34.

## SECOND DEFENDANT'S ROY GEAN, JR., RESPONSES TO INTERROGATORIES AND REQUESTS FOR PRODUCTION OF DOCUMENTS

INTERROGATORY NO. 1: Please state whether or not your fee agreement with Lois Druyvesteyn was an hourly agreement or whether it was a contingent fee agreement.

ANSWER NO. 1: Objection. The information requested is a matter of privilege between second defendant and his client, Lois Druyvesteyn. The defendant also objects to the standing of the plaintiff to question the reasonableness of the fee.

INTERROGATORY NO. 2: If your agreement with Lois Druyvesteyn was an hourly agreement, then please state the total amount of hours that you spent working on Lois Druyvesteyns' matter.

ANSWER NO. 2: Objection. The information requested is a matter of privilege between second defendant and his client, Lois Druyvesteyn. The defendant also objects to the standing of the plaintiff to question the reasonableness of the fee.

REQUEST FOR PRODUCTION NO. 1: Please produce a copy of any log or record of hours that you kept telling the hours that you spent working on behalf of Lois Druyvesteyn.

ANSWER TO REQUEST FOR PRODUCTION NO. 1: Objection. The information requested is a matter of privilege between second defendant and his client, Lois Druyvesteyn. This defendant further objects to the standing of the plaintiff to question the reasonableness of the fee.

REQUEST FOR PRODUCTION NO. 2, INTERROGATORY NO. 3, INTERROGATORY NO. 4, which all dealt with fee agreements, contingency fees, hourly rates were met with the same objection and reasons as above stated.

The Law Firm of Gean, Gean and Gean is run by the patriarch, Roy Gean Jr. who we have been dealing with on these cases. One son, Roy Gean III, has now taken over the case in the defense of his father and has complained to my attorney Troy Gaston. Troy answered his complaints by letter as follows:

Dear Mr. Gean:                                    **Feb. 27, 2012**

I certainly understand your objection to some of the Interrogatories that I have propounded in our case. I agree that they are unusual requests; however, I believe that they are discoverable in the present case. Clearly, this litigation rises out of and the facts are relevant to Mr. Roy Gean Jr's representation of Lois Druyvesteyn. I would note that I do not believe that the objection privilege is covered. Specifically, nothing I have requested would require Mr. Gean Jr. to provide the details of any advice that he gave to Lois Druyvesteyn. The details of what work was performed are not privileged so long as the same will not reveal confidential advice. Please consider providing me with the details of the fee agreement or I will have to file Motion to Compel.

-Troy

Mr. Gean III then asks the court for a protective order seeking protection of attorney billing records which he maintains is privilege information between attorney and client. Troy therefore, must respond to said motion.

## RESPONSE TO MOTION FOR PROTECTIVE ORDER

1. Plaintiff would hereby incorporate his previously filed Brief in Support of Motion to Compel wherein the Plaintiff clearly argued that attorney billing records and fee agreements are not protected as confidential communications of legal advice to client.

2. Further the Second Defendant, Roy Gean Jr. raises a number of irrelevant arguments. The Plaintiff in this action has brought this action under constructive trust. The Plaintiff has made allegations that Roy Gean Jr. was advanced money by a debtor or Plaintiff and that the same was in violation of the Fraudulent Transfers Act unless it can be shown that Roy Gean Jr. provided value for the funds he received. The

issue in contest is whether or not Roy Gean Jr. was actually owed the sum in excess of $100,000 or whether any actual value was provided to Lois Druyvesteyn in that amount.

    3. Further, Mr. Roy Gean Jr. cites law that is in contradiction to the case law between these very parties. Specifically, he argues that fraud is necessary for the creation of a constructive trust. This court is well aware by now that mere mistake or injustice is all that is required for creation of a constructive trust. That mistake may be made by a third party. The fact that the mistake can be made by a third party is evidenced by the Court of Appeals decision in this case where the Court of Appeals found that Donna Young's mistake was sufficient grounds for a creation of a constructive trust between the parties Lois Druyvesteyn and Terry Druyvestein. In the present case the only reason that any money was ever paid to Roy Gean Jr. was the result of a mistake.

WHEREFORE, the Plaintiff prays for an Order of this Court denying the relief requested in Motion for Protective Order and for all other relief to which he is entitled.

Troy follows up on **March 21,** by requesting Judge Cox to set a hearing date at the court's earliest convenience on our Motion to Compel.

I complain to Troy about the generally uncooperative attitudes of the defense parties and how the judge seems to let things go on.

Troy emails me back on **March 26.**
"I think the point that they both miss (especially Mr. Gean) is that we are suing under a specific Arkansas statute which allows us to make a claim against a third party if our creditor (Lois) had money transferred to those creditors without compensating them for it. In Linda's case, she has admitted in her own letter that the money went to her. But she has not produced one shred of proof that she spent the money on Lois' healthcare, even if that was a defense which I don't think it is. I do not

think that we should bring anything about Lois up. I think it plays to our benefit for it to appear that Linda was taking advantage of cashing checks on her poor mom."

On April 19, 2012, Judge Cox finally sets a two-hour Motions hearing for May 17, 2012, two months after all of these motions. But then I should have been happy I got a date. Mr. Gean III had a conflict so asked for a further delay. The hearing was then scheduled a month later on June 14.

On **July 11, 2012**, I email Troy.
"I am hoping that Judge Cox will rule soon and then set a trial date." I have a trip planned for Oct 6 through the 15th. Hope it can miss those dates; however, I took out travel insurance in case it can not be helped."

Troy responds that at the hearing, Linda's attorney Paige Young said they were going to propose a Motion for Summary Judgment. (Summary Judgment would dismiss the case outright.) Troy talked to the judge on another matter and as a follow up to that will ask when he expects to rule.

I question what the summary judgment is based on. Same things as brought up before?

On **July 25**, Troy responds:
"In short they are saying that we cannot have a fraudulent transfer act claim regarding the property because it happened before the court case was filed and too long ago. That is probably true, but that will not impact you in the long run if we win. The reason is that Arkansas law grants an automatic judgment lien against real property and we can foreclose on that lien (sell the duplexes) so long as Linda is not living in them.

I have no clue why the judge is not doing anything. I have never in my career had a judge take this long to rule on a motion. All I can think is that perhaps he is waiting for the defendant Linda to file this

Motion for Summary Judgment and he is going to rule on both at the same time.

I must say, the longer this runs the more anxiety I feel. I am still convinced we are right and even if we have to appeal to show the judge that (again) we should win in the long run. But this is just giving Linda more time to spend down assets! I am very frustrated as I am sure you are."

Yes, I am frustrated. It is now 2012, we filed suit five years ago. Talk about enough time to spend her mother's assets down!

# CHAPTER TWELVE
## The Case with Linda

For reasons of clarity I will separate the two cases we now find ourselves with – the one against Roy Gean, Lois's attorney and the one against Linda Van Divner, Lois's daughter. I will continue in this chapter with the case of Linda and proceed in the next chapter with the case against Roy.

On Aug. 7, 2012, we get Judge Cox's decision. I am happy he finally ruled in my favor and denied the "Motion to Dismiss" filed by Linda. We can now proceed with the case against her and hopefully finally get some satisfaction for this long legal ordeal.

On Aug. 28, Troy sends a message to Paige Young, Linda's attorney.

"It was my understanding that you were awaiting the judge's determination on your Motion to Dismiss before you would comply with any and all discovery in this case. I note that the judge has denied your Motion to Dismiss; therefore, we would respectfully request that you comply with any and all previous discovery requests. I note that you and your client have had sufficient time in which to prepare your answers and also to gather any and all evidence requested; therefore, I am requesting that your response be forwarded to my office no later than three days after receipt of this letter."

All right, let's get this thing moving. It's been 21 days since the judge's ruling and nothing has happened.

In mid-October we finally get some answers to our interrogatory questions of Linda. I list some of them because many are Objections on the grounds of attorney client privilege. Evidently Paige Young is planning to continue on from the same page of the playbook which had been used by Mr. Gean when he still was Lois's attorney.

> Question: State the total amount of money which you contend that you have paid out to satisfy medical bills of Louis Druyvesteyn?
> Answer: I have paid out $151,222.
> Question: Identify the medical provider to whom you have paid medical bills on behalf of Lois Druyvesteyn.
> Answer: I paid monthly living expenses of $139,440 for assisted living to Olathe North Homestead, and $9,030 in supplemental medical insurance premiums to Arkansas Blue Cross Blue Shield and about $2,000 for prescription drug coverage and $752 in life insurance premiums.

Now I am not an attorney but I look at this – living expenses of $151,222 for an apartment in an assisted living place and expenses for insurance premiums etc. and I wonder, "What does this got to do with me?" Lois took what the court says was actually money which was to go to my family and Linda is saying it was spent on her mother's living expenses – expenses incurred when they knew the money was being claimed by my family. So, too bad it is gone now, I spent it on her living expenses and she has now died so you are just too late. In the mean time Lois gave Linda all of her cash, her duplexes, house etc. etc. which was available for her to use for her mother's expenses but she is spending the bond money which did not belong to her. Good Lord, do you really have to be a judge and a legal mind to sort through this?

We are finally able to depose Linda (in person) on Dec. 11, 2012. I will give you some of the deposition only as it is long and a lot of it has little to do with actually resolving the case. My attorney Troy is asking the questions.

> Question: Have you reviewed the Roy Gean Jr. billing that was recently sent to myself and to Ms. Young on August 17th?
> Answer: Yes.
>
> Question: And it is like eight pages long?
> Answer: Yes.
>
> Question: And it details 566 hours of billing?
> Answer: Yes.
>
> Q: Let me just ask you generally first, is there anything, in going through that, which stood out to you or surprised you?
> A: Yes, what surprised me is what he put down, the hours that he put down. The whole thing, you know.
>
> Q: Did some of it seem excessive?
> A: Very excessive.
>
> Q: I want to specifically ask you about an entry – and at any point if you want to look at this copy, let me know. (We will get you another copy.)
> A: Okay.
>
> Q: I'm asking you, that on August 5th of 2009, Mr. Gean has entered billing to reflect that he had a phone call with you that lasted for four hours. My question to you is whether you recall ever having a phone conversation of that length with Mr. Gean?
> A: I never talked to him that long.

Q: What would you say is the longest period of time that you spent on the phone with Mr. Gean?

A: It could be 10 or 15 minutes. It wasn't that long. I mean, that would be the maximum, you know. A lot of them were five minutes you know. It's never that long.

Q: You indicated in previous responses you sent to Judge Cox, before Ms. Young got involved, that when the check from Summit was divided, that you asked Mr. Gean for a detailed billing?

A: What is a detailed billing?

Q: I'm not saying that you got one. I am asking you to clarify your statement in your August 31st, 2011 letter which says: "I asked Roy Gean Jr. for a statement of services, which I assumed would explain why he retained the $103,205 but I have not received any such statement to date." So I am asking you, what response did Roy give you when you asked for a detail of his services?

A: Let's see here. I asked for – at the beginning of the deal – I asked him how much Mom owed them. And he says, "Oh, don't worry about it." And then when we won the first case you, know, I said, "Well, how much does she owe you?" He just said "It is a lot."

Q: He just said "It is a lot"?

A: Yeah, and after that, it was all that was ever said. So when he took the check, you know, he didn't give her no billing, no nothing.

Q: Do you think that when you got your part of the $208,000 check that at that time, again, based on what you wrote here, that you asked him then, "I would like to have a detailed breakdown of your billing"?

A: No. When he took the check, you know, I thought it was weird that he had her sign the check and then he took it. I told my husband, I thought that looks kind of weird. He just came up here to Kansas and then up and took it. I thought the check was coming from the judge. That is where I asked Roy to ask the judge if the other half could be put in my name. (not Lois's name) That is because at the time we were trying to spend down Mom, because when you have an elderly, and I was advised by the doctor to do that. And then you have three years or five years when things go in your name to try to get her on Medicaid. That is why I asked him to ask the judge on that, you would think, "Well he is your lawyer, he should know the legal odds of that."

(My notes: Quite a relationship to have with your attorney. Roy takes half of the check, and does not give Linda a detailed or even any kind of bill. Linda is intent on hiding the money in her accounts so her mom does not have money to pay her bills and needs to be put on Medicaid. They call it "spending down" her mother's assets. Take her cash, take her duplexes, take her house and behold – she no longer has money left to pay her bills – much less money to pay back what they took from my family.)

Q: Was there to your knowledge, any contingent fee agreement between your mom and Roy? And a contingent fee agreement is one of those agreements you sign with your attorney that says he will get a percentage of the money should he win the case for you?
A: No. Nothing at all. (No written agreement of any kind.)

**(My notes: This was a key question because if there were a contingency agreement Roy would not be allowed anything as he lost the case. The way it was he got over $103,000 for losing a case. Not bad wages I would say.)**

Q: Now, with your copy of Mr. Gean's recent itemization of his bill in front of you, I would like to ask you some questions. On page 4, with reference to the date of March 30, 2009. There is reference to a four-hour phone call to you. Above that there is a call for three hours on March 3rd and above that there are two more phone calls on March 3rd to you. Those are for three hours each. Now, look above there and add for me the number of hours that Mr. Gean is reporting that he spent on the telephone with you that day?

A: There is no way.

Q: Let's go a little bit further. How many hours is Mr. Gean reporting that he spent on the phone with you that day?

A: Actually that is more hours than what a (work) day brings.

Q: That is kind of where I was headed. He says he spent nine hours on the phone with you, didn't he?

A: Uh-huh, and I do work.

Q: I am going to give you my phone so you can use it as a calculator. Start with the nine hours Mr. Gean claims he spent on the phone with you. On that same day, how many hours does he report that he used reviewing the depositions.

A: Eight hours, for a total of 17.

Q: Then how much time does he report that he spent reviewing the file pertaining to Summit Brokerage?

A: Eight hours, for a total of 25.

Q: And do you agree with me that there is another entry for eight hours to review the exhibits of Summit Brokerage?

A: Yes, for a total of 33.

Q: Now also add two hours for a telephone call with me, Troy Gaston, and the six hours shown to review documents filed by Terry Druyvestein, and five hours for a call to Jamie White.
A: Jamie White? He's my tax man!

Q: What is the total now?
A: 46 hours.

Q: Has your tax man, did Jamie White ever bill you for a five-hour telephone call with Roy Gean Jr?
A: No.

Q: What date do you notice that Mr. Gean places on the review of documents filed by Terry Druyvestein?
A: March 3rd.

Q: What date does the document have on it as to when it was actually filed?
A: April 6th.

Q: Of 2009?
A: Uh-huh. So you can't bill for that, if it hadn't been filed yet. Is that right?

Q: I guess, unless there was proof that they had been given to Mr. Gean earlier (which they were not). April 6th is quite awhile after March 3rd isn't it.
A: Yes.

Q: Did you review the documents and correspondence that came in on your mother's case on a regular basis? Like when I would write a letter to the judge, would you get a copy of that?
A: No, not really.

**(My notes: Roy's accounting of time and charges is entirely made up and in addition he did little, if anything, to keep his clients informed. Anyone, even Linda, can see this is bogus. There is no way Roy can justify the charges he has made for the work he performed.)**

Q: I would assume that your position is that if any more money is generated, that you have spent X number of dollars on your mom's care and that you don't owe money to anyone. Is that an accurate statement?

A: Yes.

Q: So, if Roy Gean overbilled and the Court rules that my client, Mr. Druyvestein, is not entitled to anything, do you want Roy Gean to pay any of this money back to you or your mom's estate?

A: What are you saying? If money came back?

Q: Well let us just say it this way. Do you think Roy has overbilled? He has billed for more time than he actually spent working on your mom's case.

A: Yes, he did! Yes, he did!

Q: And if Mr. Druyvestein is not awarded any of that money, do you think Roy Gean ought to be able to keep it?

A: No.

Q: Is it your position – would you rather, and I'm not asking legally who should have it, I'm just asking from your point of view—would it be more right, if Roy has overbilled, would you rather him get to keep that money he has billed for or for Mr. Druyvestein to receive it?

A: Probably Mr. Druyvestein.

**(My notes: Well, at least Linda now sees Roy as a major culprit in this matter.)**

Q: I would like you to go back to 2007. I would like to establish a starting point, what assets your mom had in her name at that time.
A: In 2007?

Q: Yes, you can just think of it as the time when Humpy died if that is easier.
A: OK, when Humpy died. Probably at that time she had the duplexes and she received one bond which was given to her. Then she bought – and then she took that bond and the money that she had and bought the house up in Kansas.

Q: That is the one that we all agreed—there is one of these bonds that should have been made out to Lois, right?
A: Right.

Q: You are telling me she cashed that one in and bought a house up in Kansas?
A: That is right.

Q: What happened to the house in Kansas?
A: She still has it – well it's in my name.

Q: Okay. When did it get transferred into your–
A: I think in the first of October of – I think it was 2007.

Q: Were the transfers to the duplexes done at the same time? A: Yes.

Q: And was this done with an eye towards Mom is eventually going to wind up in a nursing home and we need to spend her down?

A: It was. The doctor advised me after the surgery to put her assets in my name, that with her health and if she had to go to a nursing home – it used to be three years – now it's five years before the Medicaid will pay for it. You know, with her dementia and stuff like that, they can live a long time and it would take a lot to take care of her.

Q: Did she ever become Medicaid eligible?
A: No.

Q: Because the transfers had taken place too recently?
A: It has to be five years, and she was in the assisted living for almost four years.

Q: When you gave me your responses to discovery, the first date that I've seen that shows Olathe North Homestead getting a check from you is dated October 30th, 2007. Does that sound right?
A: Probably.

Q: Obviously. Some time passed from then until you got the check from Roy Gean that you deposited into yours and your mom's account that you have used. So my question to you now is, what money did you use from October 30th of 2007, until the proceeds of this case came into your account?
A: A lot of times I would use the rent money.

Q: Rent money from the duplexes in Fort Smith?
A: Uh-huh.

Q: And you are aware, that on June 16th of 2010, that the Supreme Court, or the Court of Appeals in Arkansas reversed Judge Cox's decision and said, no, that money doesn't belong to Lois, the judge made a mistake, that money belonged to Terry. You're aware of that?

A: Yes.

Q: And did you do anything on June 16th of 2010, or upon receiving notice of that decision, to segregate out any of those funds or did you continue paying your mom's care out of those funds after that date?

A: At that date I was advised by Roy Gean to take my mom to bankruptcy.

Q: And did you do so?

A: I went to a couple of attorneys, like Roy advised me, and I was shocked, shocked about it. The attorneys told me, well, you don't take somebody unless they are bankrupt, or somebody is, you know, sick.

Q: You were shocked because Roy told you to do that?

A: Yeah.

Q: And going back to my original question, I'm taking your answer to be that when you get notice of this decision of June 16, 2010, and talk to Roy, you don't do anything at that time to pull money out of the bank and segregate it?

A: No, no. No, no.

**(My notes: Interestingly, Linda makes no effort to separate the monies which she now knows are not hers to spend. She is also initially using monies from the rentals in Fort Smith to pay her mother's living expenses. This is as it should have been. Also Roy's advice is a shocker when other attorneys advise her that one does not file for bankruptcy if they are not bankrupt. Duuuh!)**

On Aug. 2, 2013, we receive a 21-page Motion to Dismiss. This motion from Linda's attorney, Paige Young, is full of law and full of repeated information. It would drive you crazy to have to read it. I will just summarize what is now claimed. There are 16 points of law that are addressed and most are based on the premise that defendant Linda did not act fraudulently nor did she hold any funds which were fraudulently obtained. She claims that for Plaintiff, in order to have a claim under the statute providing for creation of a constructive trust that either Plaintiff has to have a relationship with defendant or that fraud be committed. She also claims that Plaintiff was irresponsible because he had not posted the supersedeas bond, holding the money in the court, that Plaintiff bore full responsibility for any loss of funds as none of this would have come about had he acted responsibly. It is also maintained that the Plaintiff has no direct relationship with the defendant and as such cannot claim funds which had become lawfully hers.

I believe this 21-page Motion, which includes much citing of law and many legal arguments, is meant to intimidate as much as anything. The sheer weight of the document will require a massive effort to respond to. I think of what Troy will now have to do to respond to each and every allegation and each and every point of law and all I can see is months down the road we may get to a Court of Law where my case can be made. I can also see huge amounts of time for law clerks and my attorney and I can see much more money needed to respond to this. It makes me regret that I decided way back in the beginning that this was a simple case and I did not want to allow a lawyer to get 1/3rd of the collection – so I paid for legal fees up front and financed this nightmare "out of my pocket." We are now approaching fees paid to attorneys and specialists that amount to about 1/4th of the original bond amount. A contingency fee of 1/3rd is starting to look very good indeed.

On **Oct. 14, 2013**, I email Troy as a Hearing has been set by Judge Cox. Troy:

I am wanting to make travel arrangements for the upcoming hearing on the 26th of November and need answers to the following questions:

1. Should both Loretta and I attend? Loretta was present, along with Lois, when Humpy told us how he wished the family items and the bond monies to be distributed. The only other thing I can think of is Loretta's conversation with Linda after the error was found in which Linda said, "We do not wish to take money going to your family." This testimony is in the transcript of the first trial. (This statement acknowledges that Linda knew the bond should go to my family.)

2. Should we come early so we can go over things which we might testify to ahead of the hearing? (At the first trial I got caught flat footed and did not want to repeat.)

3. I would think that my main testimony would be around the fact that Linda deflected all questions in this matter from her mother and never, never even once, were we able to get past Linda to discuss this matter with Lois. Linda and Roy Gean Jr. handled all of Lois's financial matters from the time the mistake in bond numbers was made known until the present.

Troy responds that we should both come on Sunday and meet Monday and Tuesday if needed. No meeting the morning of the hearing, which is Wednesday.

I am learning a lot about how the legal profession works. It is a brutal awakening, but is an education all the same. There is a lot of bluffing by the lawyers and a lot of threats made by making the opposition believe that "If you expect to win this case, it is going to cost you dearly." Well this is what I perceive is now happening in our case with Linda's attorney, Paige Young. Given the right timing, threatening a massive amount of legal work and then shooting a cannon ball across the bow in the form of a settlement offer is a good strategy. It tells the opposing attorney that "We are prepared to fight this tooth and nail, so before you invest a lot of time in your effort, and cost either you or your client a lot of money, you need to consider our offer in light of what we are going to put you through. So, to save yourself the maximum amount of time, because you have not started to get deeply into this yet, we suggest you seriously consider our offer now."

I am returning from visiting with family in the Black Hills, on my way back to Montana, driving across eastern Wyoming, when Troy gives me a call. "We have received an offer from Linda to settle." OK, judges often prevail upon parties to settle matters before going to the actual court trial in a last ditch effort to save trial expenses and money for the court. I don't know how this was arranged but none the less Troy has talked to Paige and says that we have an offer to settle for $40,000. Troy goes on to say that he thinks it is a good offer and that we should seriously consider it. I have a hard time getting my mind around this. The little hand is on the ten and the clock is striking 12. I tell Troy that this is a hundred eighty from where we have been going. We were last talking about getting all of the money out of Linda and letting her recoup the funds, which in reality Linda turned back to Roy for his services. She has the money in the form of property which she got from her mother. All of the hard assets Linda got from her mom are now Linda's, and what little cash Linda can now scrape together which Lois still had or Linda can access is offered to me for my family. (a measly 38 cents on the dollar) That's not counting any interest that should be paid on the money. I ask Troy what has made him change his tune on this. He says that he is afraid that I may get nothing! What? I have a hard time squaring this with what I know and have put into this effort. Troy says that he is afraid that our trial judge Cox, has ruled against us every step of the way and will continue to do so. That is a true statement and it makes me shudder some. I always thought judges to be "honest" and in search of the truth. I had not before considered that Judge Cox could be vindictive, and would rule against me just because I had appealed a decision and the Appeals Court overruled him. There still was no evidence that could be the case here, did Troy meet with the judge and Linda's attorney and know something I did not? I should have asked Troy but I would doubt that he could or would say much further. Even if I had asked him, I am certain there could be no evidence that the judge was threatening anything. Judges do put pressure on attorneys to reach a settlement and that could be what was going on.

I was suddenly sick of the entire case. I had struggled with this for years, knowing that I was in the right. I was unquestionably right – Humpy had told me in person what he wanted done with the bond. Lois was with us and also knew firsthand what Humpy's wishes were. Now here we were, six years later, and things are destroyed in my mind as to what was right, what the truth was. I told Troy I would have to think about it and call him back.

After I returned to my home in Montana, I was still unable to reach a decision. I had, of course, thought about nothing else during the drive back home. I often wonder if it is not things like this that distract drivers and cause horrific accidents. I certainly was thinking so hard that I was indeed, a distracted driver. I should have let my wife drive but like the male asshole I can sometimes be, I chose to continue driving.

On Nov. 17, I compose an email to Troy.

Troy:

I have been reviewing our case files all day and quite frankly am disappointed with the offer we received from Linda. In fact, I believe it to be an insult to one's intellect. This is how I see the case at this time and I want you to prepare a vigorous case for my family.

1. Judge Cox ruled that Linda and at that time (Roy Gean Jr.) must pay back the amount they received with interest at 5.75%. Based on the $208,830 check from summit, that amount would now be around $267,000.

2. Judge Cox also ruled that we were entitled to legal fees for the appeal.

3. Judge Cox did not rule on this but I would think that we should also receive reimbursement for legal fees after the appeal and also reimbursement for travel and other expenses to continue this never ending legal battle.

What it amounts to is that Linda should reimburse all of these costs and if she has a case against Roy Gean, she should get after it. I would think her case is very solid and she should be able to recoup most of her money. Since Roy was obviously a crook, I would hope she could get it all back. But then, she was also trying to take something which was not hers to begin with.

Is there something I am missing here? I am certainly a little put out at what has happened to my uncle's wishes. Lois knew these wishes and she saw a way to cut out a little more cash from his estate and along with her daughter and Roy, she took it. Linda may in fact be the main perpetrator. Just last week one of my sister's husbands passed away and the appreciation my Uncle Humpy would have gotten from the knowledge that his gift was indeed beneficial and completed in the way he had planned has been largely lost. In the past seven years since Humpy's passing we have all grown a lot older and can no longer fully appreciate what his gift to us could mean. I want the judge to know this. I hope we can bring an end to this continual legal maneuvering. I would believe it is within the power of Judge Cox to at least speed things up by not allowing as much time for each step and by not putting up with constant delays. I have read nothing in the files on what, actually, their defense is. All I can surmise is that they have already spent the money. Is that a valid defense?

Well, I had to let off a little steam. I know you also have been very frustrated with this case and Judge Cox's rulings.

-Terry

I am irritated with the case, with my attorney, and with myself for seemingly have bungled the entire matter. I finally come to the conclusion that I will settle for not less than $60,000. I cannot stomach the thought of rewarding Lois and her attorney Roy, for their wrongfully taking our family's bond. Linda is simply an opportunist and loves money more than she loves her mother. There are lots of families that treat their parents the same way. I call Troy and tell him I am not happy about it but will agree to a settlement of $60,000 – nothing less. Troy thinks they may take it, having talked to Paige to get this far he feels that this is as high an offer as they will accept. I say all the same – that is my decision – and I do not want nor will I entertain a counter offer for anything less, period.

Troy responds to my email on Nov. 19, 2013.

Terry:

I have been working on your case a lot over the past two days. I am worried that you are significantly over-confident regarding our chances of a victory in court. I hope that is not my fault for failing to be clear in my briefs and other writings. I am going to make an attempt to explain this in very plain terms. I stand by my advice to you that if we can get Linda to pay $60,000 and also get her assistance to fight Roy, you should settle with her.

There is a difference in an equitable case and a legal case. The last time we went to court it was an equitable case. For purposes of helping you understand this, I have come up with an analogy. An equitable case is similar to making vegetable soup. There really isn't a recipe that must be followed strictly. If you do not have any stewed tomatoes, you can use diced tomatoes and probably make it work. If you do not have peas, then you might have a bean that would make a sufficient substitute. So long as the soup generally tastes like vegetable soup, it can be a success. That is what we were up against during the last case. We had to show that, through the lens of a general fairness, that some kind of a mistake was made and that the fairest thing to do was to award a judgment to Terry.

This time around we are dealing with a legal standard. That means it is not general rules of fairness that apply but instead a very specific statute. Think of that statute as being like a recipe to make a chocolate soufflé. Even if the judge thinks that the most "fair" thing to do, given all that has gone on, is to give Terry a judgment against Linda, we could still lose if a single element of the statute is not met. It is like leaving the baking powder out of the soufflé. If one single ingredient is missing the soufflé will be a total failure, even if all the other ingredients are present.

(I don't know where this is going but I am not following it at the present!)

The statute we have sued under is called the Fraudulent Transfers Act. To win under this statute one of the things we must prove is that Lois had an intent to defraud Terry or that she knew she wouldn't be able to pay her debts at the time the money went into Linda's account. A major problem we face is that we do not have any proof Lois was competent at the time. Therefore, she could not have any intentions. It is not enough for us to say "We don't believe she was that sick," or "They can't prove that is where the money went." We have to produce the proof. And I cannot subpoena her doctors or even her medical records to trial because my subpoena power does not extend outside the State of Arkansas. This is the element of the statute that worries me most.

The next part of the statute requires us to prove that Linda did not give any "fair consideration" for the money. Linda testifies that she used 100% of the money to pay Lois' nursing home bills and the judge believes her, then he could dismiss the case and there is nothing I could do about it on appeal.

Remember, the most we can get from Linda for a judgment is around $110,000. We cannot get a judgment for the full $208,000+ because Roy took a large part of the money. I think the smart play here is to take the $60,000 from Linda and also get an affidavit from her to use against Roy Gean. If we do not have Linda's cooperation against Roy at a future trial, then we cannot force Linda to come to Arkansas and testify against Roy (because she lives outside of the state). And we could lose the case against Roy for these same problems with proof as to specific elements of the statue that I have outlined in this message. Whereas, if Linda is cooperating with us I can this week get her to sign an affidavit and a judgment in this case that will not only satisfy our burden of proof for a future trial against Roy, but also will enhance our chances on appeal with Roy so that we can get him back in court. (Judge Cox has just granted Roy his motion for summary judgment and we have filed a motion for him to reconsider.) I would arrange the settlement in a manner so that if Linda breaks her word to us and does not cooperate, we would get a judgment against her for the full amount we have sued her for. This would make certain she testifies against Roy at a future trial.

You should also understand that your statement in your message is wrong in as much as you say the judge has already "ordered" Linda and Roy to pay you the money. He did not. He ordered Lois' estate to pay you the money. And Lois died destitute. That is a big difference. All we have is a judgment against a dead woman without assets. We are trying a very complicated maneuver to get that judgment applied against her daughter. There are many more of these cases that have been lost than have been won. You also have to see the writing on the wall. For the last six years, Judge Cox has ruled against us at every turn. Only the Court of Appeals has given us any real relief. I am explaining to you in this message that if he rules against us on the technicalities of the statute, I do not think I can win an appeal against Linda.

**(My notes: Now this I can fully grasp, I don't need to miss the baking powder and still get this: Judge Cox has not been an advocate—to the contrary—he has ruled against me all the way. He thinks he was right when he interpreted the law initially and has not changed his mind even though the appeals court said he was wrong. The case was simple—a mistake was made—the judge made it complicated.)**

We cannot recover our legal fees from the appeal in this case. I can explain why but it is not possible. Same as to legal fees for the underlying case. We also cannot mention the time you've been without money and aging. The rules of evidence do not permit those things.

**(My notes: I don't get this? If a Court rules in your favor and awards you legal fees and interest dating back to the date the money was wrongfully given to that person, does not the estate of that person still owe the money? If one dies, then these debts are cancelled?)**

Please understand, Terry, that I have lived this case along with you for the past six years. I make less money if you settle with Linda because I don't get paid to go to trial. I would not recommend this to you if I was not convinced it is in your best interest. When I go to my cancer doctor I always listen to him regardless of what my own "gut" is telling me to do. He is the professional. He is the one with no emotions involved. What you are dealing with here is not the role my doctor in Houston plays for me. I do this kind of thing every day so am not as emotionally attached as you are. So my head is probably clearer.

(Troy is honest with this and it is sobering to me. He is the professional and I need to listen to him.)

We have said "no" to the point on the $40,000. I believe the offer of $60,000 is a fair settlement. You will save an additional $4,000 to $5,000 more than if the case goes to trial. If you do not want to settle, then of course I will take this to trial and I will put it on as though it is the strongest case on earth. I will not let my doubts show in the courtroom. But I feel I owe it to you to give you my most complete advice before you make a final decision.

-Troy

(I yield to the facts presented.)

On Jan. 23, 2014, The Final Order and Judgment in CV-2012-34 is made by Judge Cox.

FILED
FT. SMITH DIST.
~~Sue Hall~~
2014 JAN 23 PM 12 17
CIR. CLERK SEB. CO.

## IN THE CIRCUIT COURT OF SEBASTIAN COUNTY, ARKANSAS
## FORT SMITH DISTRICT
## CIVIL DIVISION

| | |
|---|---|
| **TERRY DRUYVESTEIN** | **PLAINTIFF** |
| VS. | **CASE NO. CV-2012-34 (VI)** |
| **LINDA VAN DIVNER** | **DEFENDANT** |

### FINAL ORDER AND JUDGMENT

**COMES ON NOW** for hearing the Plaintiff's Complaint against the Defendant

for a Judgment under the Fraudulent Transfers Act and based upon the agreement of the

parties and the Pleadings and Briefs before the Court the does find as follows:

1. The Court has jurisdiction over this matter and venue is proper.

2. The Plaintiff to this action was a creditor of an individual now deceased

knows as Lois Druyvestein. He became a creditor of Lois Druyvestein as the result of

funds that were held by an entity known as Summit Brokerage which were improperly

paid over to Lois Druyvestein when they should have been paid to Terry Druyvestein.

The Circuit Court of Sebastian County ultimately entered a Judgment in favor of Terry

Druyvestein for this sum in Case No. CV-2007-1383.

3. Lois Druyvestein, either through her herself or through her duly appointed

power of attorney Ms. Linda Van Divner, transferred the funds in question to Mr. Roy

Gean Jr. and to Ms. Linda Van Divner. Ms. Linda Van Divner received the sum of

$105,625.72. Mr. Roy Gean received the sum of $103,205.00. This Court has previously granted a Motion for Summary Judgment filed on behalf of Mr. Roy Gean. Plaintiff's Motion to reconsider is denied.

4.    Ms. Lois Druyvestein made the transfer to Ms. Linda Van Divner without receiving reasonably equivalent value in exchange for the transfer and Ms. Lois Druyvestein believed or reasonably should have believed that she was incurring debts beyond her ability to pay as they became due. Specifically, Ms. Lois Druyvestein had entered into a long term care facility and had medical bills which would make it impossible for her to pay her debts as they became due.

5.    Terry Druyvestein was damaged by the transfer of funds to Linda Van Divner in the amount of at least $60,000. Ms. Linda Van Divner is hereby ordered by this Court to pay over the sum of $60,000 within 180 days of the date of this Order. Terry Druyvestein is granted a Judgment in that sum to bare no interest so long as said Judgment is satisfied with 180 days. Terry Druyvestein is ordered to file a Satisfaction of Judgment immediately upon his receipt of such funds.

**IT IS SO ORDERED.**

_____
Honorable James O. Cox  11-26-13
Circuit Judge


_____
Troy Gaston, Attorney for Plaintiff


_____
Linda Van Divner, First Defendant


184

I think that it was best to settle this with Linda. I read the Final Judgment and can see that the judge favors Linda by giving her 180 days, half a year to make the payment, interest free. I also am amazed that the judge also uses this opportunity to rebuff us by not reconsidering his decision to let Roy Gean completely off the hook with his decision in Roy's favor for summary judgment.

As they say, "it's not over till it's over." This is not the final chapter for Lois's attorney Roy Gean Jr.

*If you wish to review the full Order Granting Motion for Summary Judgement (dated MAY 29, 2013) please scan this QR code.

# CHAPTER THIRTEEN
## The Case with Roy

So Judge Cox would not reconsider his approval of Roy Gean Jr.'s Motion for Summary Judgment. This judge certainly has not been a friend to me. This case has dragged on for almost six years, thanks mainly to Judge Cox, and everyone is getting sick of it. So as far as Judge Cox is concerned, it is over. He approved the settlement with Linda and released Roy Gean Jr. of any liability for basically stealing $103,000, give or take a few bucks. I can only believe it is the technicalities of the law that the judge has ruled on, but if that is the case how can he so blatantly rule the way he did? On what legal grounds could Roy be left off the hook? Judge Cox found them in Roy's case so I guess it was best to settle with Linda as I am afraid he would have dismissed that case also if we had not settled. So now we must appeal Judge Cox's decision again.

So, that is what we do. Troy says that the case against Roy will likely take two years. Troy favors hiring an attorney by the name of Brett D. Watson who works on appeals as his main line of work. I have no idea if this is necessary; however, I recognize that Troy is either overly busy or overly persecuted for his work on my behalf. I don't know how many times one can overturn a decision by a judge and still be able to work effectively in his court. I know that Roy and probably his son go to the same health club as Troy for workouts. Troy has mentioned that he has

186

seen Roy "at the club" and that he does not look that good. That would be a horrible thought – for Roy to pass away and completely change the legal landscape again. In any event I would think that Roy, as a lawyer, shyster as it may seem, has the money to reimburse us if we can get the Arkansas Court of Appeals to rule in our favor. Troy has said that Roy is quite wealthy. So on the 30th of April, 2014, Mr. Watson files our documents with the Appeals Court. I give you some of his arguments.

## STATEMENT OF CASE

This is a fraudulent-transfer case in which the circuit court granted summary judgment even though the moving party offered no supporting proof. Here is the background: H. J. "Humpy" Druyvesteyn died and left his nephew, Terry Druyvestein, a payable-on-death account. Humpy's wife Lois claimed that Humpy left the account to her. After this court ruled for Terry, the circuit court entered judgment against Lois for the amount in the account, more than $200,000.

But when it came time to collect the judgment, the money was gone. Summit Brokerage Services, which held the account, had issued a check to Lois and sent it to her attorney, Roy Gean Jr. Gean returned to Arkansas, kept $103,205 for himself, and sent the remaining $105,625.72 to Lois's daughter Linda Van Divner, who acted on Lois's behalf during the prior litigation. Because the money Gean kept was purportedly for attorney's fees, Van Divner asked for a statement of the services he provided, which he would not produce.

So Terry filed this lawsuit contending that the transfer to Gean and Van Divner was fraudulent under Ark. Code Ann. 4-59-201 to -212 (The Fraudulent-Transfer Act) asking for a constructive trust, and seeking to recover the full amount of the judgment. Gean's fees were six times what Terry was charged on the same case and even Van Divner testified that Gean's fees were not based on the value of the services he rendered.

Gean conceded that he kept the $103,205 but argued in his summary-judgment motion that the money was based on an attorney-fee agreement he had with Lois. He didn't say what the agreement's terms were, and he didn't attach to his motion affidavits, documents, or even the supposed agreement to support his contention. The circuit court nevertheless granted summary judgment for Gean. The foundation of the order was Gean's unsupported assertion about his agreement with Lois and the work he allegedly performed.

Terry moved the court to reconsider its decision, because Gean's motion and the order were unsupported and because it was incorrect on the law. And Terry showed that, if the court had considered the evidence, it would have seen that the transfer to Gean was not for value received. For example, Van Divner testified about the billing statement that Gean belatedly produced after this lawsuit began to justify his fees. The hours were wildly excessive. For example, Gean billed:

1. 24 hours on October 24, 2007, 18 of which were allegedly spent reviewing the complaint.

2. 46 hours on March 3, 2009, including nine hours of phone calls to Van Divner, which she says never happened. Van Divner testified that she never talked to Gean for more than 15 minutes.

3. 66 hours billed on April 1, 2009.

4. 25 hours billed on April 26, 2009.

5. 36 hours on July 2, 2009, including a two-hour phone call "to Supreme Court about filing of brief" and three hours to fax a letter.

6. Multiple hours for reviewing letters from Druyvestein's attorney: three hours on March 19, 2007; two hours on March 29, 2007; three hours on May 2, 2007; two hours on May 4, 2007; three hours on November 27, 2007; three hours on June 29, 2009; two more hours on June 29, 2009 and so forth.

7. Charged for review of documents on March 3, 2009 that Terry didn't even file until more than a month later on April 6, 2009.

These are only examples. Read the whole billing statement to fully understand the extent of the excess. Despite Gean's failure to support his summary-judgment motion, the court denied Terry's motion to reconsider.

The case proceeded without Gean, and a judgment was entered against Van Divner. Terry then filed a timely notice appealing the judgment entered in Gean's favor.

## ARGUMENT

The issue is whether a court may grant summary judgment when the moving party offers no proof on key fact issues. The answer is that a court cannot. But that is what the circuit court did here.

Appellant Terry Druyvestein obtained a judgment against Lois Druyvesteyn. When it came time to collect, Lois didn't have the money. Summit Brokerage Services, which held the money, had issued a check in Lois's name. Gean drove to Kansas, had Lois endorse the check, kept about half for himself and sent the other half back to Linda Van Divner, the daughter of Lois. Terry filed this lawsuit to recover the money under the Fraudulent-Transfer Act and sought a constructive trust.

Ark. 56(c) (1) requires a party who moves for summary judgment to support his motion with proof in the form of affidavits or other documents. But when Gean moved for summary judgment, he offered nothing to support his contention that he was due $103,205 under an agreement with Lois or that he even had an agreement with her. (Because several people have the same last name I will use their first name to identify them.) The circuit court therefore, had no basis to find that Lois paid Gean for his services under an agreement or that the amount she paid reflected their understanding of the value of his services. Rather than grant Gean's motion, the court should have denied it because of Gean's failure to meet his burden of proof. This Court should reverse and remand.

**1. Because Roy Gean Jr. didn't support the factual assertions in his summary-judgment motion with proof, he didn't meet his burden and summary judgment was improper.**

The circuit court said in its order that it reviewed "attachments" to the motion, but there were no attachments to review. This is ambiguous in the least. Those are incredible findings considering that Gean produced neither a contract nor testimony about a contract. Gean argues that his "legal services contract" with Lois prevents Terry from contesting the reasonableness of the fees paid to Lois yet produces no such written document.

How then did the circuit court conclude that Lois and Gean had an agreement? How did it know that the money Gean kept reflected their understanding about the value of the services? It wasn't because Gean submitted any proof with his summary-judgment motion. He didn't: no affidavit, no discovery responses, no deposition transcript, and nothing to support the key issue: did the money Gean kept reflect a reasonably equivalent value? Gean's failure to support his summary-judgment motion with proof is basis alone to reverse and remand. This Court does not need to go any further.

Although it is not necessary to go further to reverse, the other documents in this case are telling. The reason Gean didn't attach anything to his motion is that his billing was outlandish.

(This section refers back to the hours listed in the STATEMENT OF CASE and I will not duplicate it here.)

Gean's statement is replete with excessive billing. Things that would normally take a few minutes were billed for hours. In fact, nothing on the entire eight-page bill took less than two hours, and everything was billed in one-hour increments.

In addition to excessive billing, Van Divner's deposition showed that there was no agreement with Gean. At the beginning of the previous case, Van Divner asked Gean how much was owed, and he said, "Oh, don't worry about it." After winning the first case (before losing the appeal) Van Divner again asked how much she owed. This time he said, "Oh, it is a lot." There was no contingency-fee agreement. Only after this suit was filed did Gean provide any billing records. Van Divner testified that Gean over billed and that he billed for more time than he actually spent on the case.

In summary, Gean did not support the factual contentions in his summary-judgment motion. That failure was fatal. The circuit court's grant of the motion was inappropriate and should be reversed.

### 2. The Fraudulent-Transfer Act does not depend on whether Terry Druyvestein had a direct relationship with Roy Gean Jr.

Gean's failure to support his summary-judgment motion is sufficient ground to reverse. If, however, the Court delves further, it will find more errors. For example, the circuit court refused to apply the Fraudulent-Transfer Act because Terry didn't have a "direct relationship" with Gean. But the Act doesn't require a Plaintiff to have a direct relationship with the defendant. Ark. Code Ann. 4-59-201 to 212. In fact, in almost every case, the opposite will be true: The Plaintiff and defendant won't have a direct relationship. That's because the Plaintiff, a creditor, pursues a defendant who received something from the Plaintiff's debtor. While the creditor typically has a relationship with the debtor, he usually won't have one with the defendant who the debtor transferred the money to.

The circuit court nonetheless concluded that because Terry had no direct relationship with Gean, "There is no viable theory of law by which Terry can recoup the money paid to Gean by Lois." Under this reasoning, a defendant has to argue only that he and Plaintiff don't have a direct relationship! The effect is to render the Act impotent. Neither the text of the Act nor the case law supports the circuit court's conclusion. Therefore, the circuit court's meandering discussion about whether Terry had a direct relationship with Gean is irrelevant.

### 3. Constructive Trusts are not limited to situations involving fraud or confidential relationships.

The circuit court found that "certainly, there is no fraud" to justify a constructive trust. That is a dubious finding considering the lack of evidence and the court's failure to explain why it was so "certain" there was no fraud. But even if there were support for that finding, the court concluded incorrectly that fraud or a confidential relationship is a prerequisite to a constructive trust. This Court has identified multiple other situations that can give rise to a constructive trust: duress, undue influence, mistake, breach of fiduciary duty, and wrongful disposition of another's property.

In fact, Terry sought a constructive trust in the prior case against Lois. This very Court found that a mistake absent fraud or a confidential relationship IS enough for a constructive trust. Therefore, the circuit court and its ruling as to constructive trusts should be reversed.

**4. Terry Druyvestein did not have to post a supersedeas bond before a prior appeal in a separate case against Lois Druyvesteyn to preserve a fraudulent-transfer claim against Roy Gean Jr. in this case.**

The circuit court took an unnecessary detour into supersedeas bonds, finding that because Terry did not file a bond in the previous appeal (a different case against a different defendant, Lois), that he bore the risk that Lois would no longer have the money if he won the appeal. That rationale reflects a fundamental misunderstanding about the purpose of supersedeas bonds.

Supersedeas bonds protect winning Plaintiffs' money judgments while defendants appeal; they have nothing to do with losing Plaintiffs who appeal. More specifically, if a party against whom a money judgment is entered files a bond and a stay is entered, the judgment can't be executed against him pending appeal. It has nothing to do with an unsuccessful Plaintiff protecting his right to recover money if he wins on appeal. The language of the bond rules proves as much: "The bond shall be to the effect that Appellant shall pay to Appellee all costs and damages that shall be affirmed against Appellant on appeal; or if Appellant fails to prosecute the appeal to a final conclusion, or if such appeal shall for any cause be dismissed, that Appellant shall satisfy and perform the judgment, decree or order of the circuit court."

When Terry appealed the previous case, he had been the losing Plaintiff. There was no judgment awarding monetary or injunctive relief. Why would he post a bond saying he would pay Lois money if he won on appeal? He would not. She would owe him money, which, as it turned out, she did.

Not only was the circuit court incorrect about supersedeas bonds as a matter of law, its excursion into supersedeas bonds was irrelevant. Terry's first case was against Lois Druyvesteyn, not Van Divner and Gean. This is a different case with different defendants and different causes of action. Therefore, even if Terry had to file a supersedeas bond in the previous case to protect his judgment against Lois, that has no bearing on whether Gean must pay to Terry in this case the money that Gean fraudulently received from Lois.

## CONCLUSION

The main point of this appeal is that Gean didn't support his summary-judgment motion with proof. No affidavits, no exhibits, no attorney-client contract, nothing. That should have been the end of the question for the circuit court. It should have denied the motion. The court instead accepted Gean's unsupported contentions. That alone is enough to reverse.

Although necessary for us to address because the circuit court raised them, the other issues in the court's summary-judgment order are distractions. More than anything, they show the lengths to which the circuit court reached to rule for Gean. This Court should reverse the order that granted summary judgment to Gean and remand for further proceedings.

Wow! This guy has hit all the buttons. He understands what has happened. The appeal is very critical of the judge in our case. I especially like the summary where he states, "More than anything, they show the lengths to which the circuit court reached to rule for Gean." Why did the circuit court Judge Cox do this? Was he partial to a lawyer buddy in Ft. Smith? Was he sympathetic to an old lawyer and club member who had started to decline physically and mentally and that lawyer means more to him than a guy from out of state, far away in Montana where he never has to deal with him directly? I guess I will never know. All I do actually know is that he has ruled against me from the beginning and I am not at all certain, even with these compelling arguments, that he will not make things hard for me in the future.

On **May 7, 2014**, I email Troy.
Troy:

I read the appeal prepared by Mr. Watson and must say I was impressed. I of course know nothing about how these should be handled, but I do know what happened in the case and can see that it is apparent that Mr. Watson grasped it in its entirety and explained it very well in the appeal. I do not see how we can lose in the appeal at least. Going before Judge Cox again is a different story. There should be something in the law that would preclude a judge from ruling in a related matter for the third time?

Has Linda made any effort to fulfill her agreement?

On May 7, Troy replies.
Terry:

I agree. I was very impressed with the brief. One reason that I chose Mr. Watson to help us with this matter is that he deals almost exclusively with the written word, as opposed to the spoken word which is more what I deal with day-to-day. I suspect that Judge Cox has read that brief and wishes that he had ruled differently. I am not quite as concerned as you are about going back in front of Judge Cox. I think the Supreme Court will give him very clear instructions on what to do.

I was told by Paige Young last week that Linda was going to pay us off within two weeks. If not, I will file a foreclosure.

On **Oct. 22, 2014**, The Arkansas Court of Appeals rules on our case.

Cite as 2014 Ark. App. 559

# ARKANSAS COURT OF APPEALS

### DIVISION II
No. CV-14-270

| | |
|---|---|
| TERRY DRUYVESTEIN<br>APPELLANT | **Opinion Delivered** October 22, 2014 |
| V. | APPEAL FROM THE SEBASTIAN COUNTY CIRCUIT COURT, FORT SMITH DISTRICT<br>[NO. CV-2012-34] |
| ROY GEAN, JR.<br>APPELLEE | HONORABLE JAMES O. COX, JUDGE |
| | REVERSED AND REMANDED |

## RITA W. GRUBER, Judge

Appellant Terry Druyvestein appeals from an order of the Sebastian County Circuit Court granting summary judgment to appellee Roy Gean, Jr. Appellant filed a complaint against appellee alleging fraudulent transfer and also requesting the court to impose a constructive trust on certain funds held by appellee that were acquired from Lois Druyvestein. We hold that there were genuine issues of material fact to be decided on both claims; accordingly, we reverse the circuit court's order and remand for further proceedings.

Cite as 2014 Ark. App. 559

WALMSLEY and HARRISON, JJ., agree.

*Brett D. Watson, Attorney at Law, PLLC*, by: *Brett D. Watson*, for appellant.

*Gean, Gean & Gean*, by: *Roy Gean, III*, for appellee.

\*If you wish to review the full Court of Appeals document, please scan the QR code.

On Oct. 27, 2014, Troy writes to Roy Gean III, the attorney for and also the son of Roy Gean Jr.

Dear Roy:

Today I received a telephone call from Terry Druyvestein's attorney Brett Watson. Mr. Watson notified me that the Arkansas Court of Appeals had reversed Judge Cox's decision and remanded the case to the trial court. Apparently, the only issue which they found that is still open is a question of whether Roy Jr. contributed equal value in exchange for the sum that he received for attorney fees. In other words it is my understanding of that ruling that if Mr. Druyvestein can prove at trial that $103,295 of fees were not incurred, then he will be entitled to judgment for the difference in the value contributed and the amount received. I told Mr. Watson that before Mr. Druyvestein makes any decision about how to move forward on this case that I would like to have an opportunity to communicate with you. I have regretted from the beginning of this case that I have had to take the position which is adversarial to your father. He has always been extremely pleasant and kind to me. But at the same time I feel as though he put me in a very awkward position in as much as I had an ethical dilemma of my own of whether to report to a client that I believed that another attorney had billed excessively. If I had not notified Mr. Druyvestein of the same then I think Mr. Druyvestein could have had a claim against me as well as a possible ethical violation on my own part for failing to represent my client due to the fact that I had a pre-existing relationship with your father.

You may recall that at the outset of this case I told you that I was willing to stipulate that Roy's contribution to the case was valued at $25,000. That is in spite of the fact that there are facts in the record to show that I only billed and collected the sum of $17,000 for my own work on this part of the case. I have spoken to Mr. Druyvestein and he is willing to accept this compromised amount which would be $78,205 in order to settle the case. Please provide me notice within ten days of the date of this letter as to whether or not your father would be willing to pay that amount in exchange for a Release of Claims.

Assuming that he is not then I will have a conversation with Mr. Druyvestein and Mr. Watson about how they wish to move forward with this matter.

Well, the last Saturday of October is opening season for big game. Mainly for elk, which has been a passion of mine since moving to Montana in 1964. I am not successful very often anymore as I am now 79 and probably not as agile as I used to be. Anyway, I go out to an elk camp made up of lifelong friends and usually no one gets hurt. The elk don't get hurt and so far none of the hunters have gotten hurt, so I call that a successful hunt.

When I get back on Nov. 8, 2014, I email Troy.

Troy:

I just got back from a hunting trip and got a copy of your letter to Roy Gean and was quite shocked to see that we were allowing Roy Gean a $25,000 fee for his services. It was my belief that we were asking for a return of our family moneys. In other words, for $103,205. What was left out of the whole offer was the fact that Judge Cox initially ordered that the money be returned to my family along with interest at the rate of 5.7% Judge Cox also ruled that we were entitled to legal fees for that appeal. I see no reason that Judge Cox will change his pattern of reasoning. Since Roy took charge of the funds on Aug. 7, 2009, the interest to date would up the amount to $138,075. Add the cost of the appeals and you get $144,775. Our offer, at a minimum should be for Roy to return the money initially taken by him which was $103,205. This offer is good till December 1st, after which I request you set a trial date. Time has passed for your initial offer to settle for $78,205 so I assume they have turned it down.

-Terry

**(My notes: I am having a hard time getting my mind around the fact that this case has dragged on for over seven years and finally we have won on all of the appeals and Roy has been dragging his feet every step of the way, causing delay after delay by appealing any**

decision all the way to the Arkansas Supreme Court. One can appeal a decision but if you lose, why does the clock quit ticking and you start the game all over again? I give you another example:

If you were to get some money from a bank by mistake, and if you then say to them, "I really shouldn't have to pay you this back, and if you try to get it back I will take you to court and I will appeal if there is any decision against me." After seven years you lose all your trial court and appeals court cases and there are no other courts to which you can appeal. Do you think the bank would settle with you and only make you pay their principal back? Especially when a judge in the past ruled that the interest rate for the money should be set at 5.7%. Give me a break. There is something wrong with this scenario. No wonder lawyers drag things on and on. They are not penalized for their delays. Especially this guy who has falsified records, lied, and in general done everything legally (and illegally) to delay, without any consequences. In addition, Roy took a lump sum fee of $103,250 for "winning" the initial case. This was obviously meant to be a contingency fee. There were no hourly billings, no nothing. So why does the court award him reasonable attorney's fees? If you take the case on contingency and you lose, you get nothing. Especially when you have done nothing but lie about the whole billing process, making fake hourly charge records, etc. If anyone other than one of the "brethren" had done this they would be in jail.)

On Nov. 8, a Saturday, Troy emails me back.
Terry:

Unfortunately, that is not how the appeal decision works. The Supreme Court ordered Judge Cox to determine the fair value of Roy's services and to award you the difference in that amount of money and the $103,250. So under no circumstances can that add up to $138,00 or $144,000. It will definitely be less than $103,000. You will have to pay an expert witness to testify on the issue and that will cost significant money. Likely over $5,000. Then there is the travel expense. I went over

Roy's work carefully and I believe he can justify $25,000 in fees. Judge Cox could probably give him a little more than that and I would not be able to get it reversed on appeal. I know this is complicated but the way the law works. Roy is a creditor to Lois and is entitled to keep the money for time he spent. Just not the whole amount.

So we can press this if you want. But I believe you will not do better than the offer and also you will have to spend money to get there. I agree this is not fair. But I can't change the law. And we have taken it to the highest court in Arkansas and this was their ruling.

-Troy

Well, I don't protest anymore and let Troy's offer stand but it is not accepted by Roy. So it is up to Judge Cox, Roy Gean III, and Troy to settle what reasonable attorney fee Roy has coming to him so they can determine what should be paid back to me. It was decided that a "Special Master" will be used to examine Roy's records and come to a fair value for Roy's services. You guessed it – I get the privilege to pay half the cost for the "Special Master." Now think about that a little. Roy doctored his records to make them stretch to a fee justification of $103,250. If the fee had been properly supported by Roy's records, we could have used them, but no, and now I have to pay half the cost to come up with what Roy's fee could legally be. The Arkansas Supreme Court ruled that Roy, although wrong in what was done by Roy and the Circuit Court Judge Cox, is still entitled to a reasonable attorney's fee and now to top it off, I have to pay for a "special master" to determine what that fee should be. A fee that has to come from an evaluation of a bunch of bogus records, and in addition, the special master's conclusions must be acceptable to both parties. So on Dec. 23, 2014, Troy provides Judge Cox with our Motion for the Appointment of a Special Master and also a request for Hearing and Judgment in our case. The appointment is for Bob Hornberger, Esq. and he feels 45 days should be adequate to conduct the investigation. At least this report by the Special Master is binding on both parties and when it is in the final stage, we should get a final judgment against Roy Gean Jr.

After getting an extension in time because the records from Roy Gean Jr. were not furnished in a timely manner, Mr. Hornberger files his Report of Special Master on March 9, 2015. The 45 days originally set up to do this job has now totaled almost three months. The bottom line is that Mr. Hornberger believes, to the best of his knowledge, that Roy Gean Jr. provided services to Lois Druyvesteyn in the amount of $22,860. In other words, this dollar amount represents work which Roy completed within the timeline of the original lawsuit of **Terry Druyvestein V. Summit Brokerage Service and Lois Druyvesteyn.**

Troy asks the judge to schedule a hearing for April 13, 2015, to establish the amount of a judgment to be levied against Roy Gean Jr. Troy said the judgment will be for the amount of $80,345. He is now concerned with collection of the judgment based upon the way the Geans have not cooperated in the past. It seems that Roy Gean III has the same views on this that his father has. Even though they got the money by pursuing what Lois, at least, knew to be wrong, and then making us go through all the hoops to prove that, we are now going to have to still "try and get it." This entire seven years of lawsuits had nothing to do with what was justified or what was based on the truth. The lawsuits only dealt with trying to correct the wrong which was created by Lois and Roy Gean Jr. claiming what was not theirs to claim. It was proven long ago that the bond was obtained because of a mistake, a mistake made primarily by Delta Finance. Knowing this, there is still no attitude on the part of Roy Gean Jr. to take the action to rectify the mistake, only an attitude of blocking any justice from ever being done and to do whatever legally can be done to hide and shield the estates of the ones who wrongly took the money. Where are people's, especially lawyers', moral compass to make things right?

On **Aug. 21, 2015**, I send Troy an email as I am at a loss as to why we have not collected anything after getting a judgment against Roy Gean Jr. over three months ago.

Troy:

I am concerned with the approach we are taking for the return of the monies which Roy Gean Jr. took from my family. It is OK if we can get money from the lot you told me about or any interest which Roy has in anything else, but the problem which confuses me is, "Why does not Roy just liquidate what he has and pay us the cash?" In other words, why does he not just turn over our money? Is he destitute like Lois was?

I would have thought that the funds taken by Roy went to the Law Firm of Gean, Gean and Gean. Since he was awarded $200 per hour for his time, it would appear that Roy's law firm should be on the hook to pay it off. The $200 per hour is representative of a business charge out rate which includes a portion for office, secretarial help etc. I was in business for over 30 years and our charge out rate included all of these things and I do not know of any time that our company was not responsible for the actions of our employees. So Roy's company got the check from Lois, where is that company now? I would believe that Roy's company, regardless of who is running it now, is responsible for these debts.

If Roy's company is not responsible, then Roy Gean personally is and what are Roy's assets? Does he own an interest in Gean and Gean, the law firm? Does Roy have a car, a house, a retirement fund? What do his income tax returns reveal? Perhaps I am on the wrong page with the collections we are receiving and that they are simply a preliminary payment and the majority of the funds will be paid shortly by Roy or his firm? I cannot believe that Roy does not have the funds. A person who receives $105,000 for the work he did for Lois must have received many fees from others within a short period of time, so where is it located? Seems like there are some big questions to be answered by Roy and I thought that within not more than 45 days, he had to do so. Also when does the addition of interest kick in? At the time the judgment was made or after the 45 days? Please give me your thoughts.

-Terry

On Aug. 24, 2015, Troy replies to my email.

Terry:

The interest begins on the date of the judgment. The judge gave him 45 days to provide us a list of assets. If Roy put this money in a checking account and it is still sitting there, then we will simply garnish that account and the funds will be returned. That is when we will learn about his other assets as well. I am pretty sure that he owned a mini-van but one car and one home are exempt from garnishment under Ark ans as Law.

The Geans did not have an LLC as you have imagined. Instead each of them had their own corporation set up. Or, at least Roy Jr. had his own corporation set up. I researched that issue years ago when I was deciding whom to sue. I have today verified that fact in preparation for responding to your message. If Roy had worked for an LLC I would have sued the firm. But he was his own company. That is not all that unusual for older attorneys. Since that is not an unusual arrangement in law practices there is not anything we can do about it to go after his sons.

The money in this case went straight to Roy and did not pass through the law firm. I am not just taking their word for that. I have demanded the bank statements at the end of the 45-day period. Roy's way of doing business has become widely known in this area and it is common knowledge that before his boys matured he ruled with an iron fist and once they grew up he spun off into his own corporation and didn't let them have their hands on any of his money. Unfortunately, he wasn't much more honest with his kids than he was with you.

I would be happy to have a phone conversation with you to discuss strategy and it may also be advisable so I can make sure you understand how Arkansas collections law works.

-Troy

On Jan. 18, 2016, I write to Troy.

Troy:

I have not heard from you in some time. What has progressed? What are our options? I do not see things progressing and I see Roy fading from the picture. It has been almost nine months since we got a judgment against Roy and nothing seems to get done. I do not see Roy as a welfare case with no ability to pay his debts. I have asked repeatedly, why can we not get a copy of his tax returns? Why is this not incumbent upon Roy to satisfy the court order?

On **Jan. 23, 2016**, Troy replies.

Terry:

Roy Jr. has died. We still could obtain his tax returns. I'm not sure that would do much good as it would not tell where his assets are located. I've done a thorough asset search which I believe is superior to looking at his tax returns. But the first problem we have is that we now know where your money went. It went to the federal government. That is one entity that we will never get the money back from. He paid the money to the IRS and State of Arkansas for taxes. Our next problem is that I believe Roy had set himself up pretty well, years before our case, to be judgment proof. His home was not listed in his name, his business office building was deeded to his children and grandchildren in the 1990s or early 2000s, and his financial accounts were minimal. I have been researching land transfers Roy made in hopes that we could find one to reverse if he made the transfer after he knew we were coming after him. But the only one that I have been able to find is the one that I sent you a check for already. These are all public records so it is not as though he can hide them from us. I also have searched for any business entities he might own an interest in. I even checked for those under his wife and other relatives' names to see if there was something under the table. I am worried that the money we have recovered from him before he died is likely to be all of the money we are going to recover. The real killer is the government being the transferee. If that was one of his relatives or a financial account or a creditor we could go after it. But the government is not required to return the money because they were owed the taxes.

There is not much to do at this point. Evidently we have to go after the money and the government now has that. We cannot go after the Gean family without probably filing a new lawsuit against them on the grounds of a fraudulent transfer.

Perhaps, we can claim the money paid to the IRS on the basis that it really was our family's money and therefore we are claiming a deduction from our taxes for the same amount. Won't even add interest. Perhaps I can get my congressmen involved to help plead my case? Perhaps, I need to just admit defeat... Perhaps this is finally over?

# EPILOGUE

Nine years after the death of uncle H. J. (Humpy) Druyvesteyn, I find myself at the end of my options. I have got reimbursed for legal fees, special council, expert witnesses and basic reimbursement for travel. This total amounts to about $60,000 which we got back from Linda in her final settlement. We also forced the sale of some properties owned by Roy Gean Jr., which was subsequently passed on to Troy and the final amount distributed to me and my siblings. We divided the proceeds evenly and we each got $4,231. So basically after struggling 9 years for what was unquestionably meant to go to my family, the bond amount of $208,830.72 which Roy and Lois initially received, ended up being $25,380 to our family -- we ended up a little short. I feel bad about this as Humpy would certainly be disappointed. It would have especially helped several of my brothers and sisters and had it not been held up so long it would also have been a big satisfaction to my mother. Not the money so much, but rather the satisfaction that Humpy recognized the big contribution that my dad, Tom had made, through his numerous trips to Arkansas to help Humpy get back on his feet after a bout with the bottle. That speaks volumes about our dad's love for his younger brother.

What realistic choices do I have to pursue the case further? As Troy has said, we know where the money went and that is to the IRS, and I cannot sue the government to get it back. I know that is a dead end, but I have a hard time getting my mind around the fact that since Roy used the money, which the Court has now said was rightfully ours, to pay off his past bills to the IRS, that we have no recourse to get it back from the IRS? I would bet that if Roy had paid me money that was obtained illegally from the government, that I would have to give it back to the government. What do you think? In the final analysis, it was still Roy who received money that was not rightfully his so it should be Roy, or in this case his estate, which has the problem of getting money back from wherever they need to. Why should it be my problem? This is a problem which my attorney now says has "no solution". Our Justice System, through the Court, has already made the decision and it was in our favor. So why can we not get financial satisfaction? Because the unlawfully gained money was used to pay off the IRS? If a person swindles money from a bank to pay off what he owes to the IRS does the IRS get to keep the money? I sincerely don't know the answer.

Troy has said that Roy pretty well made his estate bullet proof from creditors. Seems like a travesty of justice to me. Roy basically takes $103k from the bond meant to go to my family and pays it to the IRS for delinquent taxes. End of case? His wife is well set with their house, car and I would assume retirement investments. Troy told me early on that he thought Roy was well off so l doubt the fact that there is not a fund somewhere. His law firm to whom the check was deposited with and not to Roy Gean Jr. personally, was supposedly a shell company and has no assets. The other Gean's in the law firm would have you believe that they operate independently, but their firm goes by the name of Gean, Gean and Gean, thus creating the illusion of a cadre of lawyers available to look out for their clients, but no, from a liability standpoint there is nothing there. I think that my attorney is tired of this case and is not up to continue the battle. He has personal conflicts with the Gean family and perhaps has reservations to continue our case` with Judge Cox. I think that there is little to be gained to continue either. Judge Cox in particular worries me that I will not get a fair hearing. They all want me to go away and it appears that they will get their wish.

I would like to review how the subject of "truth" and justice enters into this entire case. Who told the truth? Who benefited by the truth? It was not always the person who told the truth, at least not in the short term.

Let's take a look at how this all started. Humpy went to his financial adviser Donna Young and asked her to make me a TOD (Transfer on Death) recipient of a Ford Motor Company bond. Initially Donna did her job and called me about Humpy's wishes and I provided her with the information necessary for her to set me up as TOD. After Humpy died she told me that if we waited until April, instead of cashing the bond immediately, we would receive full value for the bond and not take the horrible penalty Lois took by cashing her bond in right away. Then things get murky. Donna "forgets" about the April due date and says we will have to wait another six months, or until October if we want to cash in at full value. I think there is some absence of truth now, because after about four months, I receive a notice from Summit Brokerage that Lois has been notified that she is actually the legal recipient of the bond! This happens after we had set up an account in my name and had been patiently waiting for the maturity date. I get this notice with no forewarning or correspondence from Donna. So Donna has not been truthful about what has been happening behind the scenes. It strongly appears that the Summit lawyers had discovered the error in the TOD records and told Donna to hold off on everything until the conflict in records is resolved. The Summit lawyers determine that the records show Lois to be the beneficiary. Donna knows this is not the truth. She knows she has made a mistake but agrees to wait. I leave it to your judgment if the wait was for the three-year statute concerning this type of error to run its course before she steps up to speak the truth. That is what happens. The statute of limitation on this type of error is passed on July 21 and in August Summit sends the letter to Lois with the news. To me there is no doubt that these people used the law to shield themselves from the truth. The discrepancy in the documents would require exposing their clerical error and they could not let that happen as it could cost them money if they did. My attorney Troy allows them to be dismissed from the lawsuit. Donna then begins to speak the truth, both in her deposition and in the circuit court. She said she made a mistake, probably by filling in the account number after the fact. But the circuit court judge either does not believe that her testimony is the truth or he is afraid of going against the legal written document because he does not understand the law concerning an unintentional mistake. Looking back on it, if Donna had not finally come forward with the truth, we probably could never have overturned the judge's decision on appeal. So, how did telling the truth affect Donna? Well, holding up on the truth until the statute time had expired perhaps saved her and Summit a bundle by not drawing their careless bookkeeping practices into question. I do wish she had brought the mistake to the attention of all parties initially and all of these court cases would not have been necessary. Perhaps there would have been a whole slate of other ones but we may have fared a lot better. The big culprit here was Summit Brokerage and their lawyers who were unwilling to listen to the truth when Donna told it to them. They did not want to listen to anything which could expose them to some of the liability.

Now let's look at Lois and the truth of her testimony. That is just it; there was no testimony from Lois. Never had to do it! Lois was in the room when Humpy reiterated what he wanted to do with the bond, how he was leaving it to me and that he knew I would "do what was right" with it. So, even though Lois knew the truth, her actions speak loudly in that she certainly was not going to step forward and speak the truth. She conspired with Roy Gean Jr. to get what they thought they could by claiming possession of the bond and this caused a lot of anguish and heartache for me and my family. In addition, Lois acted quickly in shielding her assets from the truth. She at least was a participant in transferring property to her daughter Linda. And how did this benefit Lois in the end? It certainly benefited her estate but I doubt that she personally benefited that much. If only she had testified to the truth, all of these court proceedings could have been avoided. This is not to mention that she would be buried by her former husband and Humpy would be peacefully buried by his wife Bobbie. I wonder now, how that situation is going. Do you think people's spirits can make things right? Hmmm! I can only hope.

How about Roy Gean Jr? There's no debate on this one. Roy never spoke the truth because it was of no use to him, even if he had the ability to recognize it when it was in front of him. I do not know if it was because he was an attorney or if he just was so eager to get his hands on the bond money that he completely ignored the truth. It seems implausible to me that Roy did not realize the truth, that simply a mistake had been made. But that is not how the legal system works. An attorney must put up the best fight possible for his client. I have no qualms about that but I have great misgivings about all of the lying that Roy did to justify his exorbitant fees and also his hiding of all of his assets from any judgment in the future. Both of these actions speak loudly that Roy had no regard for the truth. Did Roy benefit by not telling the truth? You bet your sweet butt that he did. Outside of having to put up a very vigorous, but sloppy defense, Roy got to keep most of his ill gotten gains. The court even allowed him to make up a new bill for his services which was a travesty of justice, and all he gave back was $25,380. The rest he shielded by making his estate "legally out of reach." This in my view makes the whole justice system, both judges and attorneys, look very bad indeed.

How about Linda, the daughter of Lois? At first blush it would appear that Linda was well trained by Lois. An apple does not fall far from the tree they say. Linda initially told my wife that they "do not wish to take your bond monies." She later would say, "Talk to my attorney Roy Gean Jr. about that." I think Linda primarily found herself in the situation where she was the windfall recipient of her mother's estate and she was deathly afraid that Lois' living expenses were going to deplete too much of it. Who knows what her motivation was, but if she could add to her estate by taking the bond, which she knew was not hers to claim, so much the better. She was the recipient of all of Lois's estate.

Her duplexes, her home, her cash, her other bond and who knows what else. She was very intent on "spending down" her mother's net worth and getting it transferred into her name. She was very concerned about the five years she would have to pay for her mother's expenses before she could consider the properties safe from the Medicaid people. Linda was intent on transferring properties to shield them from any future lawsuits, either by the government or by our lawsuit which she was totally aware of from the beginning. Linda was using the law to hide behind to get her mother's properties out of reach.

Linda, along with her attorney Roy Gean Jr. were remarkable in their maneuvering to never let Lois submit to a deposition. They prevented this from happening for over four years. Toward the end of Lois's life, Linda got a doctor to say that Lois was not competent to do a deposition or to appear in court. I find that rather unbelievable as she lived in an "assisted living" facility and not a nursing home. I don't think people in assisted living are incompetent and are unable to answer questions. Another "untruth." I have to wonder if all this court fighting was beneficial for Linda. I am certain she had a lot of legal expenses. First she paid, or rather Roy Gean Jr. just took, about half of the bond money for his fees. Then she had to pay another attorney Paige Young an unknown amount to keep her half of the bond account, and in the end had to pay $60,000 to settle with my family. I guess that this shows one how money, especially illicit money, just "flies" away. In Linda's case she paid Roy $103,000 and with our $60,000 plus her attorney, I would say she paid out at least 175 or 180K for attempting to gain ownership of the bond worth 208K. Well, I guess that is better than my family did. So, by not admitting what was true she made a good profit. This does not include the inheritance of property from her mother which she was intent on hiding from the government. I can only hope the IRS audits her tax returns.

I have to mention my wife, Loretta. Now Loretta is a "straight shooter." The fact is she is too straight of a shooter. Loretta tells the truth and when she says that Linda told her that "We are not trying to take your money," that is what was said. I will give you an example of how Loretta thinks and as such everything has to be correct. This is a hypothetical example of an interrogatory.

> Question: So were you there when your uncle Humpy took Terry aside and told him specifically what to do with the bond?
> Answer: Ah…no.
> Q: No?
> A: Yes.
> Q: But you previously told me that you were there, correct?A: Well, yes, but Humpy did not take him aside, we were at the breakfast table!

So, you have to get your details right and then you will get the right answer.

Judge Cox is an interesting study. He had no financial interest in our case. He was in it entirely to do justice. Judge Cox was intent on doing what the law said. He had little focus on finding out what was the "truth." Troy made our case under THE LAW OF MISTAKE AND CONSTRUCTIVE TRUST. This statute provided for returning money to a first party, by means of a constructive trust when such money was "unjustly" given to a second party as a result of a mistake by a third party. This, in our case, resulted in an "unjust enrichment" of the second party. Judge Cox never could understand the "mistake" part. He liked to look only at what the letter of the law revealed in the TOD document, what the document said, not what the people who filled out the document were saying. A "mistake" was a concept he did not want to address. Had he looked more for the "truth" rather than at the legal letter of the law, the wrong law at that, he would have been led to the conclusion that with the help of the truth, justice could be done. Did Judge Cox benefit from the truth? Had he been more astute in looking for the truth he certainly would have benefitted by avoiding two obviously embarrassing appeals court decisions. I really have to question his ruling to allow Roy Gean

Jr. out of the case. The Supreme Court also makes me wonder how they were thinking and if they even knew all the facts in the case. They ruled in our favor but then told us we needed to pay Roy a reasonable fee for his services. Roy obviously took the case with Lois on a contingency basis, thus collecting the outlandish fee of $103,000. He then tries to lie about it, saying that he had a "regular contract" between attorney and client. He makes up bogus hourly billing records to show it is a regular contract. To his dismay, these are questioned and shown to be absolutely false and made up. The court says, "OK, but we still should pay him a reasonable fee for his services." Why? When businesses engage in this type of behavior, courts are usually ready to slap them with "punitive" damages in order to persuade them not to repeat or do it again. I would think especially in the legal profession the high courts would want to preserve an image of fairness and truthfulness, and not to perpetuate one of rewarding a shyster lawyer for unreasonable and unethical charges. The way Roy handled his clients and corresponded with them was in itself unprofessional. It made no difference in the end however, because Roy hid all of his assets "behind the law" anyway.

Now we have to deal with my attorney, Troy. Troy started out wrong when looking for the truth. Perhaps it was because he had to deal with Lois previously in a lawsuit for Jon Rose. Troy was fixated on the fact that Lois was not an honorable person. Lois would cheat, steal and lie to get what she wanted. There were also rumors from Humpy's friends and the Rose family that Lois was out to get Humpy out of the way. There was no evidence that she did all of this intentionally or from a crime standpoint; however, she did things not in Humpy's best interest. Anyway, Troy initially was fixated on a case whereby we would claim that Lois exerted "undue influence" and/or incapacitation of Humpy to coerce him to change the TOD on the bond. Troy did however, make a major breakthough when he searched the law for statutes which supported our known grounds for the case, and those were based on what the "truth" was. The truth was that a mistake, either intentional or unknowingly, had been made. Troy did come around to this truth and did a fair job representing my family's interest. Unfortunately, I believe that when he did come around there was not enough time to properly prepare our original case – a case we may not have lost had we been entirely focused on the truth.

I am disappointed that Troy did not pursue Summit harder. The fact that they stalled till the three-year statute of limitations had passed before telling Lois that she was the rightful owner of the bond is too much to pass off as a coincidence. I do not doubt that the legal staff of Summit would have been a formidable foe; however, I wish we would have tried to expose them for their legal maneuver. Perhaps we could have taught them a lesson.

Troy also had pressure, I am certain in the form of fellow lawyers and judges. You do not sue a fellow attorney in the small city of Ft. Smith, Arkansas without everyone knowing about it. Especially when you know all of the attorney's family and go to the same health club the "older attorney" goes to. Troy once mentioned that he saw Roy Jr. at the club and that Roy did not look that well. I also wonder about Troy's relationship with Judge Cox. I would ideally believe that there is not a problem with judges holding grudges against young attorneys; however, I don't see how it can be completely ignored. Troy had to appeal two of Judge Cox's decisions and we had a specialist, Brett Watson, prepare the appeal for the personal case against Roy. That, in a layman's opinion, was a very blistering rebuttal of the judge's legal thinking. Anyway, did Troy benefit from the truth? First I think he tried to always tell what was truthful and handled himself accordingly. Second, he always charged me a fair and detailed billing, nothing like Roy's. I think Troy made one big error early on in the case and that was not talking to me about what could be done to hold the bond money in trust with the court until the appeal had been processed. As it turned out we won the appeal but the money was gone and we spent all the rest of our time chasing this money. If you know what the truth is you must have confidence that you will prevail. I do not think Troy had confidence that we would prevail in the appeal. He did not have confidence in the legal system to uphold the truth. He knew that the legal system is not based on truth, only on what is legal. I, on the other hand, was naïve and had great confidence that the truth would prevail in the appeal. Had I known then what I know now, I would not have been that confident.

In the final analysis, I have to look at myself to see where I went wrong. I have the final say as to when I have had enough, where I think I should have said more or evaluated things more closely. In the very beginning, Troy asked me how I wanted to handle the payment for services rendered. He gave me the option of putting a retainer up front and then paying bills on a monthly basis which would essentially be based on an hourly fee schedule. Another alternative would be to have the services paid for with no upfront money nor any financial risk on my part. The law firm would instead be reimbursed with a percentage of the money which we expected to get back from the lawsuit against Lois. That percentage would be one third of the total. My thought at that time was, this is a "no brainer". I thought that agreeing to pay close to $70,000 for simply going to a one-time court case and laying out the facts would be way too much compensation for any law firm. Troy had also said that typical litigation of a onetime fairly simple case would run between 12 to 15 thousand dollars. Like I said, a no brainer, or so I thought.

I thought in the beginning that this must be a case of a simple mistake. A mistake which could be identified and easily corrected. This thought was supported initially when Donna Young set up an account for receiving Humpy's bond moneys. Lois had also expressed her concerns and was supportive of her knowledge that we would get our bond moneys. What I did not understand is that there is no such thing as a "simple mistake". I did not realize the difficulty it would be to get to the truth. I also came to think that perhaps someone intentionally made a mistake. Was it Lois? Was it Donna Young and Summit Brokerage? They had much to gain by covering up a mistake. There was a suspicious air about the entire delaying and execution of my uncle's directions.

An attorney often works on a percentage basis, and I can see that there is merit to this system. All sides are not of a mind to find out what the truth is. All sides do not have the same goal. What is the truth? All

214

sides have their own agenda and their own opinion of, not the truth, but what the law allows. All the attorneys have their own client to represent, what is right and wrong is not the objective here, the objective is to give the client the best representation in the eyes of the law. In this case the judge are those eyes. The attorney's job is then to suppress anything detrimental to the client and to bring any facts favorable to his client to the Judges. attention. His job is to clearly convince the judge that what his client wants is the justice the law provides. It is up to the judge to determine what then is the "truth", with respect to the law.

I have always felt that our taxation system should be structured to make everyone pay some taxes. No matter if one has only a very modest income, one needs to pay a modest tax. The main point is that "everyone has to have some skin in the game". It makes a person appreciate when we all have participated to help each other, that we all have contributed. We have ownership. We try harder.

This thinking can also apply to hiring a Lawyer. I basically believe that it should not matter, however; being realistic, it seems that is how the system works. The attorney may work for you the best when that person has the greater financial incentive to perform at his or her highest level. The attorney is working for you but has that person bought into the project? In fact, getting paid depends upon the attorneys' efforts and his professional performance. The thought is, will the attorney work harder for you under a commission or under an hourly rate? You have to decide. So, I decided on the hourly rate, but I wonder if I decided correctly?

Would Troy have worked differently if I had hired him on a percentage basis? Would it have made any difference? Would Troy have come around to the realization that it was a mistake which caused this mess? Would he have changed his approach and zeroed in earlier as to who was to benefit from this mistake, or also who would be most damaged by the exposure of this mistake? I guess I will never know, but it was in the 12th hour when Troy dropped his belief that records were changed because of "undue influence", exerted by Lois and switched to the belief that it was a case for the LAW OF MISTAKE

215

AND CONSTRUCTIVE TRUST. I give credit to Troy, who worked diligently as we neared the first trial to study the facts of the case and come to this conclusion. I wonder; however, if it would have made a difference, had he discovered this earlier? If he had skin in the game, would he have been more focused and open to other options. There is also the thought that one sees these things in the rearview mirror better than perceiving them ahead. I missed many things which were laying ahead and hindsight is indeed much clearer. On the other hand, I found out a lot of things about our system of Justice, and how difficult it is to find and communicate the "truth".

I am indeed so relieved and grateful to accept the verdicts and battles which we ultimately won. What is actually the "truth", is that we finally did win. Through the findings and rulings of both the Appeals Court and the State Supreme Court we got the system to declare the "truth". That is very satisfying and in itself rewarding for our family and to the memory of our Uncle Humpy. Justice, perhaps, was not completely administered but the "truth is what sets us free".

I rest my case

I started this account of a true happening in my life by telling you about a judge some 2,000 years ago. He asked a defendant who was accused of "lying" because He had said that He was a King, "Are you then, a King?" The man answered, "For this I was born, I have come into the world to bear witness to the truth, everyone who is of the truth listens to my voice." Pilate responds, "What is Truth?"

It was the legal position of the Jews that Jesus had broken their laws by claiming to be the Son of God and King of the Jews. Jesus was eventually sentenced to be crucified for telling the "truth." It is no wonder that "truth" can be hard to find.

*The Druyvestein Family*
*Mike, Don, Terry, Virginia, Donna, Karen*

**END**

218

www.ingramcontent.com/pod-product-compliance
Lightning Source LLC
Chambersburg PA
CBHW071555210326
41597CB00019B/3253